SELWYN
Every Day with Jesus

SELWYN
Every Day with Jesus

by
JOHN PETERS

Waverley Abbey House,
Waverley Lane,
Farnham,
Surrey, GU9 8EP

NATIONAL DISTRIBUTORS
Australia: Christian Marketing Pty Ltd., P O Box 154,
North Geelong, Victoria 3215
Tel: (052) 786100

Canada: Christian Marketing Canada Ltd.,
P O Box 550, Virgil, Ontario, LOS 1T0
Tel: 416 641 0631

Republic of Ireland: Merrion Press Ltd.,
10 D'Olier Street, Dublin
Tel & Fax: 773316

Malaysia: Salvation Book Centre, (M) Sdn. Bhd.,
23 Jalan SS2/64, 47300 Petaling Jaya, Selangor

New Zealand: CWR (NZ), P O Box 4108,
Mount Maunganui 3030
Tel: (075) 757412

Singapore: Alby Commercial Enterprises Pte Ltd.,
Garden Hotel, 14 Balmoral Road, Singapore 1025

Southern Africa: CWR (Southern Africa), P O Box 43,
Kenilworth 7745, South Africa
Tel: (021) 7612560

The publishers are grateful to the assistance of Carolyn Richardson in the
preparation of this manuscript

Typeset by J&L Composition Ltd., Filey, North Yorkshire
Printed in Great Britain by Billing & Sons, Ltd., Worcester

ISBN 1-85345-040-5 Hardback
ISBN 1-85345-041-3 Limp

Contents

INTRODUCTION

. . . turning setbacks into stepping stones

One dark night in South Kirkby in Yorkshire, an unkempt and distressed man appeared in the vestry of the church where Selwyn Hughes was minister. Selwyn just didn't know what he should do. He had not been trained in counselling, and helping people through their difficulties was not a skill that came naturally to him. The man poured out his troubles. He had a deep personal problem that was causing him extreme distress. All Selwyn was able to say was, 'I will pray for you.'

The next morning, the man's body was fished out of the canal. The post mortem revealed that he had been dead for at least eight hours. When Selwyn heard the news, he was devastated. Kneeling on the floor in his study, overwhelmed with grief, he pleaded with the Lord to so equip him that in future he might be able to counsel others. 'From that day to this,' Selwyn declared, 'I have striven, by every means possible, to develop counselling skills and to address people at the point of their need.'

Selwyn is now one of the UK's foremost proponents of Biblical counselling. The distinguishing feature of his approach is an absolute belief in the Bible being divinely inspired and without error. To this, he adds a discriminating use of secular therapies. The goal of all his counselling is to move the counsellee from self-centredness to Christ-centredness. Responding positively and constructively to need, he is constantly striving to improve his ability to help others, turning setbacks into stepping stones.

Selwyn is the founder of Crusade for World Revival (CWR). A dapper, dark-haired Welshman in his early sixties, he has that particular nation's gift for oratory, even rhetoric, but in his preaching, lecturing and writing, as with all aspects of his life (especially his use of time), he is a careful, balanced man. Indeed, had he not learned to become an astute manager of his time and energy, he would not have been able to continue writing edition after edition of *Every Day with Jesus*. He frequently quotes, with evident approval, the words of John Wesley, 'Never be unemployed, and never be triflingly employed.'[1]

He goes about his work with a calmness and a discipline that enables him to cope with a punishing schedule. It's an approach which is beneficial to those who work with and for him. These qualities are truly the fruit of the Holy Spirit's dynamic work in his life, allied to which is his clear understanding of the ways of God in both the general and the specific shaping of his life. This point is made in the issue of *Every Day with Jesus* published to coincide with the opening of Waverley Abbey House:

The beautiful thing about knowing and understanding the ways of God is that once we begin to look at our difficulties and circumstances through this particular lens, life takes on a completely new perspective. It changes from boredom and emptiness, profitlessness and purposelessness, to meaning, direction, hope, encouragement and deliverance from despair.

As I look back to the early days of CWR and reflect on God's leadings, I clearly remember some situations when I was at the point of panic – simply because I did not know or understand the ways of God. I used to say to myself: 'What is God doing? Why doesn't He do this, rather than that? What possible purpose can the Lord have in taking us down this road?' If I had been better acquainted with the ways of God, and knew them as well as I do today, many frightening situations would have been robbed of their terror. I saw His *acts* but did not understand His *ways*.

After I gained some insight into the way God likes to do things, and came to terms with it, I entered into the experience of what someone has described as 'the leisured heart'. Those who knew me well said: 'What has changed you? You were fussy, aggressive and easily ruffled – what has made the difference?' I had the joy of telling them that I had begun to understand something of God's ways, and with the understanding had come a deep inner security and peace. Many are living strained spiritual lives, and though there can be *many* reasons for this, by far the commonest is this – we are unfamiliar with our Father's ways.[2]

Selwyn ranks among the most influential contemporary British evangelicals. His wide range of contacts, both here and throughout the world (notably in America), in the key areas of counselling and preaching, have greatly helped the effectiveness of CWR's ministries.

As a widely respected counsellor (he prefers the expression 'people helper'), Selwyn is able to deal skilfully and sympathetically with a wide range of emotional problems, especially those relating to marriage difficulties. In this respect, his advice is firmly based on his personal experience of over 30 years of happy marriage to Enid, upon his constant awareness of God's creative work in his life and upon his genuine desire to help people grow to maturity and fulfilment.

Selwyn's book, *Marriage As God Intended*, has helped to heal and restore many, many marriages. One couple had decided to part, and the wife was taken in by her minister and his wife, even though the only place she could sleep in was the study. Unable to sleep one night, she noticed a copy of this book near her bed. She read it right through from start to finish, realised where her marriage had gone astray and returned to her husband.[3]

Another minister had been counselling a lady whose marriage was on the point of total breakdown, but nothing he said was effective. The situation began to change when the minister, in his own words, began to say things she found both helpful and constructive. When she told the minister this, he said, 'I've been reading Selwyn Hughes' book on marriage.' She asked for a copy, got one almost immediately, and her marriage was repaired.[4]

Many marriages, too, have been restored on the weekend Marriage Enrichment courses at Waverley Abbey House, and, again, it is worth recording that these courses developed out of Selwyn Hughes' own experience. As he put it: 'In the early days, my marriage wasn't bad enough for divorce, but it wasn't good enough to be described as marriage either. Flying back from overseas, God spoke to me, over Heathrow Airport, that my main ministry was to my wife – to be a priest in the home. So I decided to make my marriage a strength, not a weakness – and I did.'[5]

Selwyn's ardent attachment to Enid was tested to the full during the years of her final illness. She died in 1986. What enabled him to face the stress and tension was due to this insistence that *she* was his most important ministry, not his preaching or lecturing, nor even the work of CWR. Frustration there certainly was, because he had invitations to minister from all over the world; but having made the basic decision that Enid was much more important to him than any of his other commitments, he looked after her with steadfast love and deep care.

His behaviour and courage during this time greatly impressed his close colleagues and associates. Jeannette Barwick, his Personal Assistant, recalls that he visited Enid *every* day while she was in hospital. He would sit holding her hands, even when she was unconscious, for hours at a time. Jeannette also recalls his physical weakness after his wife's death but not depression, and that Selwyn could face the anguish of his own feelings and depth of grief and still get on with the many and varied responsibilities facing him.[6]

Selwyn Hughes is also a highly respected preacher. A recent article in *Renewal* (May 1988) conjectured that he may be the preacher with the largest daily congregation in the world. Whether this claim is entirely accurate when compared with the congregations of the American media evangelists is difficult to substantiate one way or the other. What is beyond doubt is that he enjoys the largest *daily* congregation of any British preacher. This is due to the fact that *Every Day with Jesus*, daily notes designed to aid personal revival, probably go into more homes worldwide than any other comparable Bible Study notes, with over one hundred and twenty thousand going into British homes. The notes are read in at least 126 countries, with CWR distributors in Australia,

Canada, Malaysia, New Zealand, Singapore and South Africa.

These notes started originally as a give-away and continued to be so for some eight years until, eventually, a charge was made. By 1989 circulation had reached over 200,000; by the end of 1990, it is estimated that this figure will increase by 100,000. In addition, there are notes for young people (*Every Day with Jesus for Young Christians*), volumes entitled *Through the Bible in One Year*, plus numerous books on Bible characters, the life of Jesus, as well as many other books and booklets.

An interim insight into the effect of *Every Day with Jesus*, which will be considered more fully in a later chapter, may be gleaned from two letters, representative of many thousands sent to Selwyn. The notes consistently meet people's needs:

Thank you so much for your notes and your latest edition of EDWJ. I have just sat down and read it from cover to cover – I could not put it down as every page spoke to me.

Tears of relief streamed down my face as I realised that it is not a sin to feel lonely, that just because the Lord is always with me I do not need human companionship. Now the guilt has been removed, as has the guilt of feeling hurt when misunderstood, even and particularly by my closest friends. Even though I know that Jesus felt all and more than any of us can ever experience, I couldn't relate this to myself, and too many of Job's 'comforters' have frequently told me that I was wrong to feel lonely, hurt, etc., but I did feel misunderstood and despised. Now I feel a burden has been lifted and my heart sings for joy. God bless you in your ministry and thank you for your so very personal sharing of the things of God.[7]

This woman's husband had left her for another woman:

I follow your notes EDWJ. On October 18th you expounded on Ecclesiastes 3:11, 'Everything beautiful for its time.' It meant a great deal to me personally. I thought when I married my husband in 1974 that he was a Christian like myself. Subsequent events proved otherwise.

I still love him and my heart aches but the notes of that day made me realise that God's pattern often comprises black and grey threads as well as the gold and silver. I had never seen it so clearly.

Life seems dark at the moment but I do believe that He will make everything – even this – beautiful in its time.[8]

Selwyn's achievements are tremendous, especially when it is realised that he did not have the advantage of a university education, still less an Oxbridge one, whose theological training was fairly rudimentary and whose ministerial career, before his work with CWR, was spent in largely unknown churches in Cornwall, Yorkshire, Wales and London.

Today, Selwyn Hughes, Trevor Partridge and David Rivett direct the operations of CWR from the elegance of Waverley Abbey House, near Farnham, which has a history stretching right back to 1128 when a group of French monks planted the first Cistercian monastery on English soil. In the 19th century, the house passed into the hands of George Nicholson, brother-in-law of Florence Nightingale, who was a frequent visitor to it. So, too, was Sir Walter Scott, whose Waverley novels took their name from the abbey.

This building was described in *Renewal* magazine as the 'Hilton' of Christian training centres. The whole building has an air of efficiency and neatness, and the beautiful decor demonstrates a scrupulous attention to detail. The long-term objective is to use Waverley Abbey House as the base for a Christian university.

All of this is a far cry from the early days of CWR when Selwyn Hughes and Trevor Partridge, his partner and fellow worker for the past 16 years, worked on a shoe-string. Trevor remembers those days very clearly:

Our seminar notes were pasted up by Selwyn and myself sometimes at 3.00 am. Our Weybridge offices consisted of three rooms and a box-room. Wallpaper was peeling off the walls and rain came in through the ceiling. We had to clamber over boxes of publications. The desks were bits of wood held together.

Out on the road, we'd eat at the local fish-and-chip shop after a seminar. If we had nowhere to stay, we'd go to a small hotel, but not before 10.30 pm, so we could negotiate a lower price. We'd explain that we needed accommodation but not at their normal rates![9]

The rise and development of CWR and the phenomenal growth in the numbers reading and subscribing to *Every Day with Jesus* are two of the remarkable stories of 20th century Christianity. How, then, did the present situation come about? To begin to answer this question, Selwyn's story must be traced back to his early days in Wales. There, as we shall see, foundations were built into his life which have run like golden threads throughout the last 60 years, and which prepared him for the work and outreach of CWR. These include loyalty to the Word of God as a guidebook for everyday living, a consistent prayer and devotional life, the absolute importance of the family and a consuming interest in revival:

> In 1965, I founded the Crusade for World Revival with the primary objective of encouraging people to pray for both personal and corporate revival and deepen their understanding of the Word of God. Other goals and objectives have been added to these over the years, but the primary goal is still that of helping God's people prepare for revival.[10]

These aspects are brought together at the start of this biography because they pinpoint a fundamental perception of Selwyn Hughes' Christian faith: *it is relational.*

Chapter One

THE EARLY YEARS: WALES AND BIRMINGHAM

. . . in the dawn of Revival

Selwyn Hughes was born at a distinctly uncomfortable period in the history of South Wales – 27th April 1928, just ten years after the end of the First World War. Soldiers returning home to Britain in 1918 had been led to believe that homes 'fit for heroes' would await them. They found nothing of the kind. There were not enough jobs to go round. The fortunate few who found employment received poor wages that had not kept pace with inflation; morale was low.

At that time coal mining was the principal industry of South Wales. From 1920 onwards the miners – then the most vociferous and powerful men in industry – were enraged by the continually falling wages, and, in 1926, took part in the General Strike. The beautiful valleys, stretching from Cardiff northwards to Brecon, were torn apart by frustration and bitterness, as well as by the ravages of the industrial revolution.

Nestling high in the hills of Fochriw, about three miles from Dowlais in the county of Glamorgan, stood South Tunnel Terrace – a row of small cottages like many hundreds of others weaving their way through the stark grandeur of the valleys. This is where Selwyn was born – the first child of John Wyndham Hughes and his wife Lily.

John Wyndham worked in the local coal mines, though he was not himself a miner. His specific responsibility – a vital one – was for the electrical wiring of the pit. The more important part of his life, however, had nothing to do with the mines. Still less was he concerned about political campaigning. His heart lay with the Assemblies of God mission hall where the family worshipped. He had no hobbies: he lived and breathed the Church and the Christian life. In awe of God, he sometimes carried his puritanism to extremes: no football on a Sunday, while even cooking was out on the Sabbath: Sunday lunch was prepared on Saturdays!

Despite these austerities, Selwyn received a warm welcome into the world: 'Loving hands received me, and carried me as soon as was convenient to the little Pentecostal Church nearby to be 'offered back to God' or, as you might say, *dedicated*. At the time this was something of a local custom and he was, doubtless, surrounded by a joyful crowd of relatives and friends.

Family ties meant a lot to the Hughes'. Lily Hughes, like her husband, came from a large family – the sixth of 12 children. Though a committed Christian, she was a little less strict than John Wyndham – and she particularly enjoyed visiting the cinema. Her support for the local church was enthusiastic, and today she still attends the Elim church in Bargoed.

As a small boy, Selwyn was the only child in the family. His sister, Pamela, did not arrive until much later, when he was a teenager. His earliest memory is of listening, while lying in bed, to his father praying. God was taken seriously and His Word was revered; this made for a strong sense of security, despite the shortage of money. Though the first five years of his life were filled with poverty and strict economy, they were days of deep spiritual power which left their mark upon his life. He grew up and developed in an atmosphere of simple trust and dependency upon God.

The Hughes' would attend church together, and John Wyndham would sometimes preach. Like many of his contemporaries, he was a fiery preacher. It was in the church that Selwyn, as a small boy, spent some of his happiest moments – though his idea of fun would almost certainly seem strange to today's children:

As a child of five, I used to think it fun to sit with my cousin in the Old Ambulance Hall, used as a Pentecostal church, and watch the people receiving the baptism in the Holy Spirit. First they would sit quietly, listening to the preaching of the Word, and then, at the invitation to 'receive', they would inhale and exhale violently like a steam engine building up pressure until, in one violent explosion, the stream of 'other tongues' would come rushing out. I would wait for this wonderful moment and dig my cousin in the ribs with the remark, 'Another Puffing Billy off!'[1]

Pentecostalism and Stephen Jeffreys

Against the backcloth of depression and gloom, there was a burst of vigorous spirituality in the valleys: drunkards in the public houses were struck down under conviction; cripples were leaving their crutches behind in the church, and all over the mountain sides groups of believers would meet day after day for prayer.[2]

The 1920's revival was due, in part, to the ministry of Stephen Jeffreys. Converted during an earlier revival in Wales, which took place in 1904, he rapidly became an outstanding open-air preacher – while continuing to work in the mines. A little later, in 1907, he experienced the baptism of the Holy Spirit, an experience that gave him great power when he was witnessing to people about Jesus Christ. In 1912, or thereabouts, Jeffreys received his first invitation to conduct an evangelistic campaign – in a place called Cwmtwrch, Swansea. It was an outstanding success, so much so that the *Life of Faith* newspaper declared Wales to be '...in the dawn of Revival'.

Just before the outbreak of the First World War, an extraordinary event caused a radical transformation in Jeffreys', already successful, ministry. While preaching on a text from Philippians, 'That I may know him, and the power of his resurrection,' it dawned on him that the congregation was transfixed. Although they were obviously listening to him, something else was happening. When he had finished the sermon, his wife beckoned him down into the hall. On the wall behind the pulpit, there was an image of Christ. Jeffreys later wrote:

There in the wall was the living face of Jesus with a Roman nose and Jewish features. His hair was like wool, parted in the middle. When I examined closer it looked as though his hair was streaked with white like that of a middle-aged man in grief. We remained in the chapel for a long time looking, and scores of others who heard about it came to examine. Among them was a strong sceptic, who declared, 'I have seen and now I believe.' He came in an infidel and went out a believer. Hundreds flocked in to see the sight, which remained for several hours.[3]

From that day on, many thousands were converted by his ministry and there were many miraculous healings.

In 1922, Stephen Jeffreys moved to Wales, where he had an enormous effect on the Pentecostal churches. He also campaigned for the newly-emerging Assemblies of God. So Selwyn's formative years were spent among people for whom Pentecost, and the baptism in the Spirit, was something new, fresh, dynamic and wonderful. Many received the gift of tongues and this spiritual language became as much a part of daily life as English or Welsh. Selwyn remembers those days with joy:

> Such glory lingered over those meetings, many of them held in barns and disused railway carriages, which left an indelible impression on my mind, such as will never be erased. I find myself longing, again and again, for the same power that characterised these services to be seen in every one that God privileges me to conduct today.[4]

Northwards to Birmingham

By the time he had reached the age of five, Selwyn was well-settled in Fochriw Infants School. He was happy among his friends and his home life was stable and secure. So when his father decided that the family should move to Birmingham, Selwyn's world was turned upside down. John Wyndham's decision had not been taken lightly: he believed that Birmingham (some 175 miles north-east of Dowlais) offered prospects for his family that were unattainable in the increasingly depressed South Wales. In this he was perfectly correct, but Selwyn's antipathy to the city was instant and violent:

> After the freedom and beauty of the Welsh Valleys, Birmingham was like the black pit of hell. Oh, how I hated the narrow streets and the smoke and the schools! I never

did settle in the City and so deep was the horror in my heart that, try as I will, I find it difficult to recall many memories of those distant days. It seems that my subconscious mercifully released me from the memory of that which I so violently disliked.[5]

Worst of all, he was unhappy at his new school, where his classmates professed complete incomprehension of his thick Welsh accent. But, looking back on that time, Selwyn believes the move northwards prepared him for later life by showing him that changes have to be adjusted to, however difficult they may be. He had to work hard at life in Birmingham, but it built perseverance into his character. He learned that he could not run away from unpleasant situations.

His pleasures in Birmingham may have been few, but he recalls with a smile one particularly amusing incident. As in Wales, John Wyndham went preaching on Sundays. He had a particular dislike for one of the churches he visited regularly, where three old ladies who sat in the front row would often go to sleep during his sermon. Normally he tended to start his talk at a relatively high pitch, and keep his voice at that level, but this time he began slowly – in a deliberate attempt to lull the ladies into a gentle doze. Once they had nodded off, he began to tell a story. Selwyn remembers it well:

It was the story about a girl called Mary trapped in a house on fire. He told the details to the rest of the congregation who were awake, in subdued tones, and coming at last to the place where the girl leaned out of the window to shout for help, he cupped his hands, leaned forward in the pulpit and with every ounce of energy, of which he was capable, bellowed 'FIRE'.

The old ladies shot out of their seats as if they were stung! Everyone laughed at their confusion. Perhaps it was mean, and I have never been able to find out whether it cured them of sleeping in church or not, but I was proud of my father that night.[6]

Back to Wales

One foggy morning in 1938, Selwyn heard the news he had been longing for: they were to return to Wales. John Wyndham's work in the Metropolitan Vickers factory had led to a build-up of lead fumes in his lungs, so it was thought it would be best for him to go back to South Wales. No doubt he was also concerned about the worsening international crisis and, with the threat of war with Germany, perhaps he was anxious to be nearer to close family and friends. Whatever the reasons, Selwyn rejoiced in the fact that they were going home.

The peculiarly Welsh longing for home (they call it 'hiraeth') was at last assuaged. For a time, the Hughes' had to lodge with Lily's parents, until they could find a suitable house to live in. No matter: they were back. Within a few months, Selwyn's newly-acquired Midland accent had departed. For a short while it had caused him great unhappiness, isolating him from the local children, who taunted him unmercifully.

The return meant that he again came under the spiritual influence of several men in addition to his father, whose example and teaching have remained with him to this day. It also meant resuming activities at the little Assemblies of God mission hall where he had been dedicated ten years earlier; and now, some fundamental questions began to occupy his thinking.

Chapter Two

CONVERTED AND CALLED TO PREACH

*God wants you to
be saved tonight!*

The year is 1944. The Second World War is five years old as Britain's relentless struggle with Germany continues. Winston Churchill's dynamic leadership is a crucial issue in the hard-fought battle between Britain and the might of Nazi Germany, but victory will not come for well over a year. The people in South Wales, no less than their counterparts in England, are weary but have not lost the will to achieve a complete victory over the aggressor.

By this time, Selwyn had spent two years at Bargoed Grammar School (1940-1942) where his name adorns the list of scholarship winners, an achievement which gave him and his family enormous pleasure. Grammar schools in those days had a reputation for their intellectual and academic excellence, and continued to be so until their replacement by the comprehensive system. He only spent a comparatively short time at the school before starting an engineering course at the Bargoed technical college. A special dispensation – because of the availability of a job at an engineering works in nearby Dowlais – had allowed him to leave the grammar school at an unusually early age. The engineering course was followed by a five-year apprenticeship in the Guest Keen and Nettlefold's steelworks.

Selwyn loved the whirr of the machinery, the heavy acrid smell of burning steel, the quick movements of the various machines and he thought, as he says in *Walking with Destiny*, that he had found his true destiny. The negative side of his experience in the steelworks was his enthusiastic discovery of a number of unattractive activities, which were singularly absent from his home:

> I learned to swear, to gamble, to dance, and, day by day, my heart and soul pursued a downward path that led away from God and all that I had been taught at home. Night after night I would go out 'with the boys' and come home to find my mother and father waiting for me. It was nothing to

lie to them to avoid telling them the truth about my nightly escapades. I don't remember the excuses I made, but they were many and varied. My parents knew I was attracted by the vast emporium of lights the devil was dangling in front of my eyes, and despite the fact that Satan was inveigling me into his lair 'prayer was made without ceasing' for me, and it was this that stayed my downward course.[1]

However, there were several other important developments and influences upon him, not least his own personal and intellectual quest for answers to life's problems.

Internal quest

At first, Selwyn took little interest in the tumultuous events of the Second World War, but later he began to take an active and informed interest in the global struggle. He also asked himself such vital questions as 'Why am I here?', 'What is the purpose of my being in the world?' and 'What is the meaning of life?' In this respect, he was simply growing and maturing in a perfectly normal way. Not especially precocious or talented, just the development of an ordinary boy, admittedly doing so, of course, against the background of a horrific war. No immediate answers or reassurances were forthcoming, and his quest was to last for a few years longer until he found the answers 'all complete' in Jesus Christ. What is significant about the years 1938-44 is that Selwyn was not to be fobbed off with artificial or unreal solutions – he had to work it out for himself with a judgement based on the facts and evidence before him. He is still the same today: in tackling a problem, he begins at the heart of the matter, not from where others would like him to begin. Take, for example, the *Every Day with Jesus* comment for 28 July 1989, in which he continues his treatment of Psalm 73:

There is a price to pay for our desire to grab at easy answers instead of facing the tough issues of life and thinking through them to more Biblical conclusions. The price is 'trivialisation'. 'Trivialisation' is the acceptance of explanations that ignore the difficult questions of life in order to experience relief from confusion. I have no hesitation in saying that this is the curse of the modern Church.

One way trivialisation reveals itself is in the acceptance, by so many, of the view that the major cause of problems in Christians is demonic activity. This view seems to be spreading like wildfire in some parts of the Christian community. Demonic activity can be a cause of problems (especially in those who have dabbled in the occult) but it is not the *major* cause. The New Testament teaches us the importance of spiritual warfare, but it has much more to say about the influence of our carnal nature on the rise and development of problems.

In the early days of my ministry, when people came to me with problems, I would frequently engage in the practice of rebuking the devil, and those prayers often brought great relief. But the mistake I made was not to sit down with the people who came to me and deal with the beneath-the-surface problems which had given Satan a foothold in their lives. By making it appear that Satan was the *only* problem, I trivialised the issue. It's a lot easier (and less confusing) to sit down with a person and 'take authority' over Satan than it is to think through together the tough and perplexing issues that lie beneath the surface, and then work towards giving some Biblical perspectives. But that is demanded of us if we are to help each other towards maturity.[2]

Example of godly men

As we have already seen, tremendous excitement was created in the South Wales valleys by the preaching and healing ministry of Stephen Jeffreys. Selwyn grew up in a church greatly affected by the revival atmosphere generated by this remarkable man, a church fully sharing his emphasis on the operation of the gifts of the Spirit and believing absolutely in signs and wonders.

Yet more direct influence on Selwyn came from three local men. At the forefront was David Thomas. Married to Lily

Hughes' eldest sister, he was a kind, genial, godly man who – like John Wyndham Hughes – worked in the local mine. He was also pastor of the church attended by Selwyn's parents from the mid-1920's until 1960. He was highly respected in the community, with a dignified and gracious bearing. He had a comprehensive grasp of the Scriptures and it was he who taught Selwyn to meditate on the Word of God. Selwyn was about ten years old when he first came across Bible meditation, and it was something that helped him not only to think God's thoughts, but also to concentrate more at school. He found his thinking expanding and he was able to grasp ideas more easily. His memory span increased, too. David Thomas taught him that if he began to understand God and His ways, then he would be able to see into the heart and essence of life itself. So under Thomas' influence, Selwyn's mind began to function more clearly and concisely.

He also whetted the boy's love of the Scriptures, lent him books, taught him the value of grasping the context when reading the Bible and encouraged Selwyn to travel from the text to the personal level of discipleship, so that the Word of God speaks personally to the mind, spirit and heart. All this went deep into Selwyn's spirit, and today he recognises the profound influence David Thomas had upon him. His uncle, too, was a self-taught man for whom Christianity was an education in itself. Another man to affect Selwyn's growing awareness of God was Dewi Morgan, an elder in David Thomas' church. He, too, was a miner whose primary interest in life was bringing people under the influence of the Gospel of Christ. Dewi Morgan was a loving personal worker, not good in the pulpit, but an eager soul-winner. Selwyn paints an affectionate portrait of him in *Sharing Your Faith*:

Dewi was my Sunday School teacher, and did as much as anyone to bring me to Christ. Unfortunately, he suffered from a slight speech impediment. Because he stumbled over his words, he had learned to cut his sentences short, sometimes to just three or four words.

I can remember his telling me on numerous occasions:

'God loves you . . . He wants you for Himself . . . He died for you . . . Give Him your life . . .' and so on.

The thing that remains in my memory to this day is the tone of voice Dewi used when he spoke to me concerning the state of my soul. It was tender, compassionate, loving, concerned, winsome and considerate. There were times when I brushed his arguments aside, but there was no way I could defend against his tone of voice. At times it haunted me. I would wake up in the middle of the night and hear the words, 'God loves you,' spoken in such tender tones.

And when finally I walked down the aisle of the church in the village of Fochriw, Glamorganshire, to receive Christ, my conversion was due in no small measure to the impact that Dewi's compassionate tone of voice had made upon my life.

Dewi has now gone to be with the Lord and when I talked recently to a man who had come to know Christ through Dewi's life and witness, he told me, 'It wasn't what he said. It was the way he said it that got through.'[3]

And there was Tom James, an elder in the church and widely regarded as a Bible teacher. A miner, he had a clear, analytical mind, and had been a part-time student in the Bible school run by the Reverend R.B. Jones in Porth, Glamorgan. Here, again, it is possible to see a paradigm of Selwyn's future development: pastor, teacher and evangelist, three strands that persist to this day.

His father's prayers

Today Selwyn is in no doubt about *when* the Holy Spirit began convicting him of his true spiritual state and his desperate need of God in his life. He was on his way to the local dance hall one evening, which meant going past the Assemblies of God mission hall where the weekly prayer meeting was being held. As he did so, thinking of the pleasures ahead of him, he heard a familiar voice – his father's – crying out to God for Selwyn's conversion. The effect on the 15-year-old was dramatic. He stopped in his tracks, quite literally rooted to the spot. 'Somehow as he prayed,' says Selwyn, 'his voice penetrated my soul.' His dilemma was a real one: what should he do? Should he interrupt the prayer meeting and tell the congregation that he wished to be saved? Or should he wait to see if the feeling would abate and eventually wear off? He hesitated and the feelings of guilt and shame passed – at least temporarily. When he arrived at the dance hall, however, his sense of enjoyment was spoilt. 'There seemed to be something odd about the whole place. The lights were not so bright. The music was not so exciting.' In fact, he felt out of place there, surrounded, as he was, by scores of teenagers, like himself, eager to enjoy the evening's entertainment. The significance of what was happening was perfectly clear to him: 'I was a soul imprisoned by the Holy Ghost. I was a convict of the Holy Ghost.'

Selwyn's conversion did not take place immediately that night – and the next three months were nightmarish. He came to loathe the Sunday services:

Oh, how I hated Sundays! What little colour there was in those coal-stained valleys seemed to be altogether bleached out when Sundays came around. It began with the sound of the local church bell pushing you out of bed on to streets as silent as the grave, broken only by the slamming of a door, the barking of a dog or the raucous voices of the paper boys as they hurried from house to house.

Sunday meant church three times a day. It seemed that no sooner were you out of one service than it was time for the next. No playing in the streets. No reading of anything except it had some religious or spiritual significance. The prohibitions were many but what made it even worse was the fact that it always rained on Sundays. At least, so it seemed to me. On this particular Sunday, in February 1944, it seemed to rain more than usual. The towering mountains on either side reached up into the black clouds scudding overhead and pierced them until every drop of rain emptied out on the streets below.[4]

He tried to achieve inner peace and satisfaction through a constant round of pleasure: music, gambling, smoking and football. However, none of these gave him real pleasure as he continued to fight against the promptings of the Holy Spirit, while David Thomas repeatedly pleaded with him to make his peace with God. What happened next is best described in his own narrative:

I never expected, neither did anyone else, that the preacher booked to preach on that Sunday night would have turned up at the local mission hall. His home was six miles away and to get to us meant a tortuous route along the top of the mountain – his only transport, an old bicycle. Quite frankly, I was a little disappointed to see him. It meant that the service would be as long as usual, and if there had been no preacher we might have got out in an hour. Now it meant that we would be in church for two hours at least! The back seat of the mission hall was reserved for our group of about six boys who sat there every Sunday evening. We liked the back seat because it meant that during the sermon we could carry on our weekly game of noughts and crosses un-observed. We would wait for the announcement of the text and this was the signal to begin the game. It finished when the preacher finished. But there was something odd about the game this night for we found it difficult to concentrate on what we were doing. Time and time again our attention kept being drawn to the platform. There was nothing particu-larly dynamic about the speaker. I had heard him a dozen times before and had never been impressed, but now he seemed to have a magnetism that reached out and took hold of our minds, almost drawing our attention against our will.

His face was irradiated with a strange light. His words seemed to have barbed edges that tore into heart, mind and conscience. 'God wants you to be saved tonight,' he was saying . . . 'come to Jesus who will save you from your sins and give you peace and joy that will last forever.' I had heard these same words a thousand times before but this night they seemed to take hold of me with a power I had never known before.

What was happening to me? The tears were coming into my eyes. The strong resistance to the appeal that I had built up over the years was breaking down. My defence was crumbling. My heart, weary and sick with sin, was crying out for the Saviour. I was being drawn by the magnetism of the Cross. As the appeal went out, I was the first to move. The church was not very long but the walk down the aisle to me that night seemed a hundred miles. As I moved toward the front my pastor, David Thomas, was there to welcome me. The same arms that had held me in dedication years before, now were thrown around me to welcome me to the fold.

I sobbed out my repentance before God and took the forgiveness He offered me through Jesus Christ His Son. Joy flooded my soul as God forgave my sin and gave me the assurance that I was born again. Oh, the happiness that filled my heart that night as I rejoiced in my new-found Saviour. I felt as if I was going to burst!

I was 'saved'.[5]

He slept that night with perfect peace in his heart, though worried about the reception he would get from his colleagues at work next day:

How was I going to tell my workmates in the engineering shop where I worked that I had become a Christian! I knew exactly what I had to do. The cigarettes must be thrown away. I was the organiser of the engineering shop football pools system and that would have to be given up. My swearing would have to stop. How could I do this? I felt too weak to even plan the methods I would adopt but I needn't have bothered for, as I slept, God was quietly planning for me.[6]

The day began much like any other day, but Selwyn found that when Jesus Christ comes into a person's life, he lives there too:

The train that took me to work puffed its way into the station at about 6.30 am. It took about half an hour on its uphill climb to the little steel town of Dowlais four or five miles away. In that half-hour, I made the greatest discovery of my life, that when a man or woman takes Jesus Christ into their life, He resides there. He doesn't just come in, then leave. He abides. I felt Him in my heart as I gave my first stammering testimony to the fact that I was saved. The boys in the railway carriage handed out the cigarettes, as was the custom, but I refused, giving as my reason that I had given up smoking because I now had something better. 'Since last night,' I told them, 'Jesus Christ is in my heart.'

There was an awkward silence. Someone tried to argue about religion but no one seemed interested enough to reply to his points. I sat in the dark carriage and prayed my first prayer that God would help me that day not to fail Him in any way.

I needn't have worried about the engineering shop. When I arrived some of the boys who had been in the railway carriage had gone before to spread the news that I had been saved. When I opened the door of the shop that morning, I found it buzzing with excitement. One of the old wags slapped me on the back and said, 'Good morning, preacher.' Another said, 'What's the topic for your sermon today?' It was all good-natured fun and I felt no malice, but it provided me with the cue for constant testimony, and, all through the day, I had the joy of telling one after the other just how real Jesus was to me.

Some couldn't believe it. They said, 'We will give you a week,' others said, 'A month.' Some said, 'It's too good to be true.' I think I finally convinced them that I meant business when I handed over the football pools account together with a letter of resignation.

From that moment they knew I wasn't joking. This was real to me and, by the end of the day, a strange atmosphere descended in that shop. The simple power of my testimony to Jesus Christ had, like yeast in a loaf, begun to work. I was introduced for the first time to the thrilling reality that God was only waiting for me to do my part and He was ready to do His.

I felt His keeping power. I knew His promise that 'to as

many as received Him to them gave He the power to become sons of God' really worked.

That night, when I lay back upon my bed, I knew that my life had been really changed. A new future was opening up for me. Christ had made the world of difference to me. I prayed that I might make some difference to the world.[7]

Selwyn's life had undoubtedly changed dramatically, and, from the start of his Christian life, the Bible occupied a centrally important place:

I walked the streets in fellowship with my unseen Friend. I knew that Jesus lived, not because someone else told me, but because, in His infinite condescension, He was living within my heart. Whenever I opened up the Bible, it seemed as if it was set to music. Carried on the crest of a boundless enthusiasm, my soul would burst spontaneously into song whenever something new would open up before my gaze. I thirsted to know the Word of God and would spend hours pouring over my Bible looking for some new discovery, some new challenge that would beckon me to rise higher on the highway of Holiness.[8]

Water baptism

The next stage in his life of faith was water baptism, in obedience to the clear teaching of the New Testament. His pastor quickly arranged the service. For Selwyn it was a thrilling experience to follow Christ in baptism 'in an outdoor baptismal pool at the foot of the mountain in which our little village snuggled'. The comparatively easy, untroubled progress to baptism by immersion was totally different from the next significant event in his Christian life: baptism in the Holy Spirit.

Baptism in the Holy Spirit

Selwyn was encouraged to seek this blessing. Christian friends told him that he needed supernatural power to be able to witness to Jesus Christ in his every-day life. It was an experience in which he would be flooded with the power of the Spirit by the Lord Jesus, in accordance with His teaching of John 1:29 and 33,[9] for example. This promise of power was particularly attractive to Selwyn as he was an uncommunicative teenager, hesitant and shy. He wondered whether the baptism in the Spirit would transform him from being a reticent follower of Jesus Christ into, as he put it, a 'fearless and flaming disciple'.

So, desperately thirsting for this dynamic, life-changing power, he went to a Pentecostal convention meeting one Saturday night where the preacher's text was, 'Have you received the Holy Ghost since you believed?' (Acts 19:2). The effect on him was as thrilling and as powerful as he had hoped for:

My heart throbbed as I listened to his fervent and fiery exposition of this text. I longed for him to finish his sermon to give me a chance to receive, but he seemed to keep on and on and on. I could hold back no longer. The soul thirst within my being was so acute that I could not live one minute longer without the empowerment of the Holy Ghost. Throwing caution to the winds, I stood up in the middle of his sermon and cried out, 'Please pray for me now. I want to be filled with the Holy Ghost.' 'Put up your hands,' he said, 'and begin to praise the Lord.' I did as I was told and, as I raised my hands and began to praise the Lord, suddenly it seemed that the heavens had broken loose above me and a wave of heavenly glory swept around my soul. Oh, the joy of this heavenly Baptism! Power flowed into my soul as I praised and magnified my Lord in languages I could not understand. For two hours, I poured out my soul in other tongues as the Spirit poured Himself into my life, and when at last I realised where I was and it was time to go home, I carried with me, from that Pentecostal church, an experience that has never left me from that day to this. The baptism of the Spirit did three things for me. It made the Bible more wonderful. It made my witnessing far easier. And it made Jesus more real and vital in my daily life.[10]

He felt a new man for whom fear and trepidation were emotions of the past:

> On my way home from the service where this happened I talked freely to people about Jesus Christ – something that I was previously afraid of doing. The next morning, being Sunday, I stepped out on to the street of the village where I lived and preached for about fifteen minutes in an open-air service at which scores of people were gathered. They were utterly amazed that the shy, young teenager they all knew could suddenly hold their attention with the story of his conversion. At work the next day, I found no difficulty whatsoever in witnessing to my workmates about Jesus Christ. They, too, couldn't get over the fact that my shyness had dissolved.[11]

Everything his friends had said became true in his daily experience. Another vital factor was that Jesus Christ became more and more real to him. His Saviour was not just an historical figure enshrined within the pages of an ancient book, but a living person who spoke personally and practically to him amidst the demands of every-day activities. This tremendous degree of power in his life, with the desire to witness for Jesus, was, paradoxically, accompanied by aggressive sinful forces which, from time to time, stirred deeply within him. It was a battle that raged unabated for six months:

> I fought hard with such things as lust, sensuality, rebellion and other things, until one night, worn down by the conflict that was going on inside me, I shut myself in my room and prayed, 'Lord, inside me is a team of wild horses that are out of control. If you can't control them, no one can. And if they can't be controlled, then I would rather die.' I was rather desperate, as you can imagine from that prayer, but that night God met with me in an unforgettable way.
>
> After several hours of waiting before God in prayer, I was given a vision of Christ upon the cross. I saw Him hanging there, and even now as I write, I am conscious that the

details of that vision were ineffaceably imprinted on my memory. I saw the blood flow out from His wounded side. I saw the spittle of the soldier upon His cheek. I saw his body writhe under the pain. Then suddenly the vision of Christ vanished, and all that remained was an empty cross. The Holy Spirit said to me, 'Now you step on the cross.'[12]

As Selwyn reflected carefully about this strange and un-nerving request, the words of Galatians 2:20 came to him: 'I am crucified with Christ: nevertheless I live; yet not I, but Christ liveth in me: and the life which I now live in the flesh I live by the faith of the Son of God, who loved me, and gave himself for me.' A few days before this he had come across Dr Daniel Steele's comment in his book, *Milestone Papers*: 'When we come to consider the work of sanctification and purifica-tion in the believer's soul by the power of the Holy Spirit, we find that the aorist tense is consistently used. The tense, according to New Testament scholars, never indicates a continuous or repeated act but one which is momentary and done once and for all.' The upshot was that Selwyn came to realise that 'just as Christ was placed upon a cross and had His life ended by crucifixion, so now I, too, was invited to enter into a similar experience. It occurred to me, as the vision stayed before me, that there was no way I could atone for my own sin as that had been fully and finally settled by Christ on my behalf.' He also realised that:

This invitation of the Spirit was to place myself symbolically in his hands so that a deathblow could be delivered to the sinful tendencies that had so deeply troubled me. In my vision I saw myself nailed to that cross. There was no pain, just a consciousness of absolute surrender. When the vision vanished, I was filled with a deep and wonderful peace. I spent the whole night in prayer, and the next day, even though I had foregone a night's sleep, I felt as if I was walking on air. Over the days and weeks that followed, I became aware that as my previous encounter with the Holy Spirit had given me a new sense of *power*, this had given me a new sense of *purity*.[13]

Selwyn reflects on this whole matter in *A New Heart*:

> When sharing this experience with others, those of the
> Pentecostal persuasion say that I received the baptism in
> the Holy Spirit when I received *power*. Those of the holiness
> persuasion say I received it when I experienced *purity*. The
> older I grow, the more I see that the Holy Spirit cannot be
> put on railway lines, so to speak, and run only on the tracks
> of our preconceived ideas. My own opinion of what I
> experienced in the light of Scripture is that they were both
> genuine encounters with the Holy Spirit. And what
> happened to me may not necessarily take place in the same
> way in the lives of other Christians. Some appear to enter
> the Christian life and receive everything all at once. They
> are saved, empowered with the Holy Spirit, and go on to
> show evidences of God's purity in their lives in just a matter
> of weeks following their conversion. Others, like myself,
> move a little more slowly through the stages. In offering the
> testimony of my own experience, I do so not that you might
> emulate it but that you might consider what I say, and see if
> it accords with the way God is leading you, and your
> understanding of the Scriptures.[14]

So by faith Selwyn offered himself to God to be crucified with
Christ, an experience of sanctification by faith which had
many practical benefits:

> What practical benefits did I gain from this experience of
> sanctification? It did not result, I found, in placing me
> beyond the possibility of a carnal thought, a stab of pride, a
> trace of envy. It meant, rather, that I became more
> conscious of the Holy Spirit's presence in my subconscious
> than I did of sin's presence. Evil was not eradicated in me
> (as some proponents of 'imparted holiness' believe) but I
> found that the eagerness for it had gone, the appetite for it
> brought under control and the hunger for it no longer a
> clamour. It wasn't that I found it impossible to sin – that
> would be going too far – I discovered, however, that it was
> possible not to sin. Temptation was still present in my life

(indeed, there is no ground to suppose that in this life we will ever pass beyond the range of temptation) but I found that I fought it with greater ease than before, and although at times there were struggles, fierce struggles, I sensed that something had happened inside me that, while not taking away my responsibility to say a flat 'no' to sin, reinforced my desire for God, bringing me out, time and time again, into complete and total victory. I was able swiftly to assess wrong thoughts in the light of the Spirit's presence in my heart, and seeing them to be evil, renounce them quickly and dismiss them as undeserving of even momentary attention. Now, close on 40 years later, I look back on that experience with feelings of deep gratitude to God, and I will never cease to thank Him for the day when, through the Holy Spirit's operation on my life, I felt His cooling, cleansing touch.[15]

Called to preach

After these transforming experiences, Selwyn had absolutely no embarrassment sharing his faith. It is something he has gone on doing ever since. In the years since then, he has come across many, many people who claim that sharing the Good News with others is interference in a person's human rights. Faith-sharing, by implication, is only done by bigots and fanatics. But Selwyn's answer to such arguments is:

Suppose someone suffered a deep cut, say, on their forearm. What is the best way to treat it? In some parts of the world there are those who would say it should be covered with cow dung. Elsewhere there are those who would say one should carry a lucky charm which will help to make one well very soon.

Most people, however, believe that the best way to treat a wound is to wash it clean and apply some antiseptic to it.

Whatever views people might have we *know* that the last of the methods I have described above is the best. It is the same with the faith we are called upon to proclaim. Just as the world has the right to know that the *best* way to treat a wound is by cleaning it and applying antiseptic to it, so does it have a right to know that the way to obtain eternal life and joy is through a personal encounter with Jesus Christ. It is not 'interfering in a person's human rights' to do that; it is plain humanity to do so.

Just suppose that some Russian scientists discovered a cure for cancer. And suppose, after having done so, they decided to keep it a close secret and apply treatment only to members of the 'iron curtain' countries. That would be a crime against the whole of humanity. The same indictment would apply if such a cure were found in any country of the world, and its leaders or scientists failed to make it known. If we, to whom it has pleased God to reveal Himself in Jesus Christ, were to keep the knowledge of His offer of eternal salvation to ourselves, then it would be a crime against the whole of the human race.[16]

Selwyn's next important milestone, a call to preach, was not a single event but a rich tapestry of several distinct, though interrelated, experiences.

He was at a rally in Crosskeys, near Newport, when he heard a missionary, by the name of Jimmy Salter, speak on 'The Call of God', based on Mary and the incarnation. The speaker pinpointed an important Biblical principle: 'that whenever God desires someone to do a special work He does not leave them to infer it from circumstances alone, but breaks the news personally. God did not allow Mary to infer her high motherhood from the changes that went on within her body,' said the preacher, 'but broke the news to her beforehand.' I can see him to this day, leaning over the pulpit and shouting into the midst of the congregation: 'Before the incarnation, there was an annunciation! Everyone has a work to do for God in this world, but if God wants you in the ministry or in missionary work, then He will not suffer you to guess, to speculate, or conjecture. He will come to you and tell you so Himself.'[17]

It was a sermon that deeply affected Selwyn. It reverberated in his mind as he travelled the three miles to work at the Bedlinog colliery where he had been recently drafted for National Service. He explains:

Between 1944 and 1947, the Government at that time decided that all young men eligible for National Service should be drafted into the pits to help the national emergency in relation to coal. I was one on this list directed into the pits. From an early age I remember my father saying that no child of his would ever go down the mine. Most mining fathers say this but, in my case, the Government thought otherwise and I began my work in the mine.

My work involved servicing the various pieces of machinery that were used to cut the coal, and because this work could only be done when the machines were not in action, I was permanently appointed to the night shift. Work started at ten o'clock at night and ended at six the following morning. Somewhere around two in the morning, everyone was entitled to a 30 minute break and on this particular morning the break time found me quite alone in a disused part of the mine. I took out the New Testament which I carried with me and, after a brief prayer, began to read. I have no recollection of the reading but almost every other detail is imprinted on my memory. I recall closing my New Testament and turning my thoughts toward the Lord in meditation and prayer. I remember also the strange, almost eerie, silence that pervades the corridors of a coal mine in the dead of night. And I recall the peculiar sigh – known only to those who work underground – that the earth makes in the early hours as it seems to sink down into sleep.

Then I heard it. A voice . . . not audible, but speaking directly into my soul: '*I want you in the ministry.*' That was all – nothing more. It would be impossible for me to convey in words the effect that moment had upon me. It is as real to me now as it was when I experienced it almost 40 years ago. Such was the power and impact in my heart that to have asked for a further sign would have been impertinent. God had spoken. I knew without a doubt that it would be just a matter of time before I would leave the coal-pit and enter the pulpit.[18]

He shared his conviction with his pastor and uncle, David Thomas. Naturally delighted by Selwyn's spiritual progress, he affirmed the young man's call to preach and promised to give him training on two evenings a week for six months. What Selwyn learned has stayed with him ever since, the principles and practices being basically the ones he uses today:

> He began by showing me that a well-constructed sermon has three parts – a commencement, a continuation and a conclusion. I remember saying, 'That's easy enough to understand but how do you know what to say? How do you gather enough material to hold the attention of the listeners?' 'First, you sit down, with a blank sheet of paper, before a text or passage on which you feel you want to comment; then prayerfully proceed to put down all the thoughts that come to you about it. Don't worry about the order of the thoughts – just get them down. Later you can give them structure and form.' He went on to give me another good piece of advice – don't consult a commentary on a chosen text or passage until *after* you have exhausted your own thoughts. 'Commentaries are fine but they can be terribly intimidating to a beginner. Get your own thoughts down first and then compare them with what the experienced Bible expositors have said.'[19]

Although he was longing to preach, he had done little of it apart from giving simple testimonies about his conversion. Nor had he made any effort to construct a sermon or expound a Biblical text. So David Thomas' training came at exactly the right time.

The day came when he was asked to preach to a group of young people in the church. Selwyn's preparations were commendably thorough. He spent a whole week preparing, prayed daily for help and was determined as he climbed the pulpit steps to take the whole place by storm. He thought his sermon would last at least half an hour, but things did not turn out quite as he expected:

> I invited the congregation to open their Bibles at Luke 17. 'The theme I have chosen for my first sermon is the

well-known story of the ten lepers.' After reading the appropriate passage I plunged into my sermon with enthusiasm. I raised my voice, waved my arms, and delivered my soul on the subject of how sad it was that as in the story of the ten lepers so many of us receive the blessings of God but so few of us show any real gratitude. After what seemed like an age, I sat down in a bath of perspiration. I looked at my watch. I had taken exactly three minutes![20]

His friends were quick to congratulate him after the meeting but Selwyn, knowing he had failed, felt deeply disappointed and humiliated. He never wanted to preach again. Gradually, however, the call to preach burned into him 'like a mighty flame'. Yet he was more in love with the sheer mechanics of preaching rather than as a way to communicate the living Christ. This problem, plus a stubborn will was dealt with through a tragic experience:

One morning during the middle of the night shift, I found myself working with a young man in a quiet and derelict part of the mine. Our job was to rescue some air pipes that were in danger of being covered by a fall of roof. It was a risky business and, as we pursued our task as hurriedly as we could, I felt impressed by the Spirit to witness to this young man. But as there was a sense of urgency about our task and we were in a little danger, I postponed it, thinking there would be other opportunities later in the night. I was wrong. A few minutes later a fall of stone weighing many tons tumbled from the roof and completely covered my workmate. I looked dumbfounded and horrified at the sight. It took me a few moments to recover from the shock and running through the dark underground corridors I went in search of help. It took ten men a solid hour to remove the rock from off the boy's body. When we finally got to him, I saw a sight that has been ineffaceably imprinted on my memory. His body had been flattened as if run over by a steam roller. Blood was everywhere. The jagged rocks had made a score of holes in his body and from each hole, I watched his life pour itself away with the blood.[21]

From that moment onwards, he vowed that he would never again be disobedient to the prompting of the Holy Spirit. He felt guilt, sadness and remorse at the tragic death – feelings that persisted for days: 'I wept and pleaded with God to forgive me for failing Him in a moment when a soul stood between life and death.' Out of it all, however, came a determination to witness constantly to the saving grace of Jesus Christ.

Influence of the Scriptures

Meditating on Genesis 22 and Romans 12 one day, Selwyn realised that, just as Abraham had offered himself as a 'living sacrifice' to God whatever the consequences might be, he, too, had to do the same. His call to preach must be accompanied by a willingness to be led by the Holy Spirit. By now he was 20 and needed ministerial training to sharpen his thinking and his understanding of God's ways. He also needed to take time to increase his knowledge of the Word of God and also learn to consistently apply that knowledge to every part of his life. On top of that, he needed to get away from the rather parochial, inhibiting atmosphere he had been brought up in and broaden his horizons. This would also make him more independent, more prepared to stand as a person in his own right in a place where he was not just the son of John Wyndham and Lily Hughes, but a man capable of making his own decisions, able to hear God for himself and to respond to His promptings.

So, in 1948, he found himself at Durham Park Bible School, Bristol, an independent Assemblies of God Bible college, later to merge with Kenley College which today is Mattersey Bible College, near Doncaster.

Selwyn spent two years at Durham Park. He had been recommended to the college by David Thomas, who had invited the principal, John Wallace, to preach at the Fochriw church. His course comprised four main sections. First, the

Doctrine of God, where the students did an in-depth study of God's character and attributes. Then, the books of the Bible were analysed, mainly by John Wallace, who had a very great impact on Selwyn, particularly with his emphasis on structured homiletics. Hermeneutics (interpretation of Scripture) and homiletics (art of preaching) formed the third component of the course. Finally, the students were given practical experience of preaching, every Sunday morning in college being devoted to the art of preaching. This was quite rigorous and demanding. After a student had finished his sermon, he would have to listen to a critique by his fellow students – not an experience for the faint-hearted! However, it was an integral part of a prospective minister's training, for which Selwyn now feels grateful.

A typical day at the college ran like this:

6.30 am	Rise from bed
6.30–7 am	Private devotions
7.30–8 am	Cleaning the college, lighting fires, etc.
8–8.45 am	Breakfast
9 am–1 pm	Lectures
2–5 pm	Work on set questions on the morning's lectures, together with discussion groups
6.30 pm	Evening meal
7.20 pm	Evening free for recreation and further study

This sort of timetable clearly shows a very important characteristic of the Durham Park approach: its emphasis on the theoretical *and* the practical. The students also did domestic duties to help keep college fees as low as possible. It all helped Selwyn to be as careful and as wise as possible as far as money was concerned. There were at least two reasons why Selwyn found the course both immensely enjoyable and profitable. There was his response to the Bible. From the start of his Christian life he had been fascinated by the Scriptures, so, at Bristol, it was sheer joy to him to be able to study the Bible in detail, free from the constraints of the daily work routine. He became, as he put it, 'lost in the wonder of the Word of God.' He learned not only to 'live *by* the Bible but to live *in* it'. He also received advice which he regards to this day as priceless:

> I was taught by a reverent use of the imagination to slip within the covers of the book and make it autobiographical. I was taught to run back through time and walk with Peter, James and John as they moved around the Saviour. To see Lazarus coming out of the tomb, tearing aside the grave clothes, and to watch the leper that Jesus cleansed. It was made clear to me that there are two ways of reading the Bible – to read it with or without imagination. You can read it from outside or you can read it from within. 'Slip in your imagination into the skin of Zaccheus,' I was told, 'and think yourself into him.' Feel as he felt. Stand up inside him and look out through his eyes and see what he saw and the whole book will become different. This advice was perhaps the most priceless advice I ever received. Put it to the test yourself. Take an incident from the scripture, climb into the skin of the person concerned and live for a day in them. You will be amazed at how those Bible characters come to life for you.[22]

There was plenty of fun too. Selwyn records an incident involving him and his Swiss friend, Andre Lemarquand:

> One of our most enjoyable moments was the night we frightened the matron out of her skin. Mrs Wright was a kindly soul but austere, reserved and very commanding. In fact, some of us thought at the time that she was a little pompous but, looking back, I think we were wrong. However, it was this balloon of supposed pomposity that we set out to burst. And this is how we tried to do it.
>
> It all began when Andre and I were rummaging about in the cellar. In the dust and darkness, we discovered a 'knight in armour'. I can't say a knight in 'shining' armour because the armour was discoloured, rusty and very, very dull. It really would have made an excellent museum piece had it been properly preserved, but immediately we saw it,

we hit upon a plan. We agreed that at the stroke of midnight we would quietly carry the suit of armour up the stairway and stand him outside the door of matron's room. A gentle knock on the door, and our sudden disappearance would leave her to be confronted by the grim appearance of this relic from the past. We did not share our plan with anyone and then, at the dead of night, we stole in the cellar and carefully carried the armour up the wide staircase to the matron's room.

We listened carefully. All was quiet. Standing the figure outside her doorway, we tapped gently on the door and scampered as quietly and as quickly as we could back to our room. A few minutes elapsed whilst matron climbed into her dressing gown, switched on the light and quietly opened the door. As we fell into bed the piercing scream of matron reached our ears. It had worked!

The next morning around the breakfast table, we saw a very distraught matron. Breakfast proceeded with the usual early morning quietness and, as soon as it was finished, matron brought up the subject of the 'knight' outside her door. Who was responsible? No one spoke. So stealthily matron began her process of elimination. She began to state firmly and categorically that she thought there were certain people there who would never stoop to such a thing. And the first one she mentioned was me!

This was too much for my friend, Andre, who sat back in his chair and laughed and laughed and laughed. This incident, of course, started the whole group around the table laughing, and I was forced to own up and confess that, even though matron had eliminated me first, I was responsible along with my friend, Andre, for her fright in the middle of the night. I thought matron came out of the whole incident very sportingly because she never mentioned it ever again. The incident was never completely forgotten though for, being one of her favourite students, I had held a place of honour by her side at the meal table. The following term, I found myself at its other end.[23]

The two years in Bristol went swiftly and Selwyn had to make hard decisions about the future. John Wallace offered him the alternative of either going to a thriving Assemblies of God church in the north of England, with a fairly good wage, plus plenty of other opportunities, or to Helston, Cornwall, where the situation was totally different. At the latter was a broken down little assembly hall with just a handful of people who could barely afford to pay the rent of ten shillings a week, yet who wanted a pastor. Obviously, the Cornish church would be a tough proposition for an experienced minister, let alone one fresh out of Bible college. In making his decision, Selwyn carefully considered the principal's advice and counsel: 'A church that's ready-made will never satisfy your spirit.' John Wallace, with typical wisdom, put his finger on one of Selwyn's chief characteristics: his pioneering spirit allied to his considerable determination. So Selwyn decided on Helston. How would he fare in his first pastorate, in a town very different from his own Welsh background? It is perhaps curious that no offer from a Welsh Assemblies of God church was made to him. The answer is found in the next chapter, which also tells of his meeting with, friendship and subsequent marriage to Enid Osmond, a Cornish girl, with whom he was privileged to share 35 years of married life.

Chapter Three

THE YOUNG MINISTER

. . . sharing Christ's love with a lost world

In July 1950, Selwyn set off on a six-week evangelistic trek with his friend, Andre, and three others. Pulling a cart that carried their camping gear, they retraced John Wesley's much travelled route from Bristol to Land's End about 200 miles away.

The trip was of especial interest because John Wesley was one of the greatest evangelists of all. He used every opportunity to present the Gospel to the people and firmly believed that any day not committed to this was a day wasted. So the five young men set off, determined to seize every chance to use their newly-acquired preaching skills.

John Wesley's writings had a big influence on Selwyn, who identified with the Methodist founder's impatience with Christians reluctant to speak about their faith. Jesus came into this world to give new life to those who will receive Him. If we neglect our responsibilities to share this with the lost and wandering, what hope is there for them? 'How strange it is,' wrote Selwyn, 'that so many Christians can be so tepid over the vital task of sharing Christ's love with a lost world.'

Helston 1950-51

All good things must come to an end. With the summer holiday over and finished, Selwyn found himself, that September, in an old Salvation Army hall in Helston for his induction service. There were twelve people in the congregation – six of them visitors from other towns. As Selwyn stood in the pulpit, preaching his first sermon to the tiny flock, he had no idea of where he would be sleeping that night, for the local church had not made any arrangements for him. 'By a miracle,' he says, 'I found a room in the house of a Christian lady who was attached to the Apostolic group, and it was from this one room that I made my plans for the development of that little church.'

His pioneering spirit flourished, and he lost no sleep over

the inadequacy of his salary. With total confidence in the Gospel, Selwyn faced the awesome task before him with all the courage and vigour that one would expect of a 22-year-old full of the Holy Spirit. On top of that, he knew, without a shadow of a doubt, that God had called him to preach. No other career would satisfy him, and he was exhilarated at the prospect of all the challenges that lay ahead.

If the congregation at his induction seemed tiny, it shrank to virtually nothing the following Sunday. Six people were there. The collection totalled 12 shillings and sixpence (about 62½p). Of this, ten shillings was already earmarked to pay the rent for the hall in which they worshipped, leaving Selwyn the rest to live on for the week. His dinner usually consisted of a couple of cups of beef-tea, costing a penny a day. 'The rest of the money,' Selwyn remembers, 'would go on tea, milk or whatever I could get cheaply.' He was kept in shoes and clothing by his faithful mother who, from time to time, sent him parcels from Wales.

Many weeks of hardship, stringent economy and great difficulty followed. Eventually, however, Selwyn's preaching on the power of the Holy Spirit and the dynamic effect of the Word of God started to break through to the people.

One night, at a prayer meeting attended by ten people, a young woman, who had recently become a Christian, began to speak in tongues. This was a surprise to Selwyn because only a few weeks before he had been talking with her about the baptism in the Holy Spirit and she had shown no apparent interest. He had evidently misjudged her, discovering later 'a great hunger in her heart to be filled with the Holy Ghost'. Selwyn was overjoyed, seeing this event as clear evidence that the Spirit was at work in his ministry.

Enid

The young woman was Enid Osmond. Born in Cornwall on 10th August 1929, she was the youngest of James Henry and Annie Osmond's four children. Because she was so petite and pretty, she was perhaps rather spoilt as a young child. Every Sunday morning, she would be seen at the Wesleyan Sunday

School in Coinaghall Street, but in the evening, she went to the Salvation Army meeting with her family. Her childhood was extremely happy until she reached the age of 13, when her mother died. It was the end of the world for her. Deeply affected emotionally, she went through a desperately unhappy period. Two years later, she left school and went to work in a Bray outfitters' shop. Three years later, she got a job at Culdrose Royal Naval Air Station. Eventually, she became the manageress of the Naafi (Navy, Army and Air Force Institue canteen) there. She was very much a typical young woman of the world at that time, fond of smoking, dancing and dates with boyfriends.

She was converted to Christ through the preaching of Pastor William Roy and, after Selwyn's arrival in Helston, she regularly attended the Assemblies of God church. Her life changed completely. Gone were the cigarettes and she now spent all her spare time attending church meetings. Selwyn, on his part, was attracted by Enid's kindness and generosity – and they soon became firm friends. Seeing that he had so little money for food, she would try to help him out with some 'little extras' from the Naafi. From the beginning, Enid was a constant support to Selwyn. Caring and sensitive, she was always there behind the scenes. Then a member of the youth group, she was of enormous help to him as he strove to establish and build up his congregation upon Bibical foundations.

Friendship soon blossomed into romance and they were married on 10th April 1951 at the Bible Christian Chapel, Meneage Street, Helston. Rev Philip Anstey, the pastor from Falmouth Full Gospel Church, conducted the ceremony. Enid was to support Selwyn unfailingly for 35 years. Her genuine interest in others and her constant concern for their welfare grew and developed. These qualities characterised her whole life. They marked her out wherever she went, in all the different stages and locations of Selwyn's ministry. All those who knew her recall Enid's personal and individual interest in their Christian lives, their homes and their relationships. Selwyn was the up-front person, with an overwhelming desire, especially in his 20's and 30's, to succeed in his various ventures and initiatives. Enid quietly got on with her own task – consistent and wholehearted nurturing of the people with whom she came into contact.

Selwyn was now backed by a group of young people filled with the Spirit and longing to work for the Lord. As he encouraged people to tithe, the coffers swelled. More important, however, souls were saved and God's power flowed into many lives. The growth of a church, Selwyn discovered, is in direct proportion to the enthusiasm inspired in its members. Encouraged by Selwyn's eagerness to win people to Christ, the small congregation sought to reach others themselves, 'each one reaching one'. 'Where this emphasis is upheld,' says Selwyn, ' . . . no church can fail to increase its size, double its membership and become a force and a power for God in the community in which it is placed.'

Selwyn's year in Cornwall was an invaluable experience, giving him the chance to put into practice the theory that he had learned at Bible college. He was able to develop his preaching skills week by week – something he could not have done in such a short time had he gone straight to a larger church where there was more than one minister. Beginning his preaching career in such a discouraging situation meant a wholehearted effort to enlarge and stimulate the congregation. His determination to succeed was crucial. On the pastoral side, he resolved, from the beginning, to face the real facts of a situation head-on and refuse to opt for any 'pat' or easy solutions. This quality was to bear rich fruit in the early days of CWR, although, at that time, in the British church at least, the art of counselling was then in its infancy. Selwyn realised, however, the vital importance of helping people to face up to their problems – whether emotional, physical or psychological – rather than allowing them to fester on, creating even more problems in the long-term.

Trusting God each day for the material needs of his life, Selwyn proved for himself the truth of Paul's words in Philippians 4:19, 'And my God will meet all your needs according to his glorious riches in Christ.' He learned, then, to be content with what he had; as a result, wealth and possessions have never featured high on his agenda. If Christ's word is dependable in each and every situation of life, what more could one possibly desire? Finally, of course, there was the fact that it was at Helston that he met and married Enid who was to give him all those years of unswerving support. With Enid at his side, he was perfectly content. Soon they were ready to take a new step into the future. 'I set out,' Selwyn recalls, 'to follow the Spirit's leading, that would take me into many strange and unusual places – and ultimately to settle in the place of destiny to which His guiding hand would lead.'

Llandilo 1951–53

The call to Llandilo, near Carmarthen in west Wales, came in 1951, in the wake of an evangelistic campaign by Howell Harris. Howell had been invited to Llandilo by Ernest Griffiths, a local chemist. The effect of the evangelist's preaching, followed by Selwyn's faithful ministry, led to the establishment of an Assemblies of God church with a congregation of about 50. Selwyn also became pastor of the Pontardulais church, near Llanelli, which had a similar number and which had been without a minister for a time. Selwyn experienced a more satisfying response to his ministry than in Cornwall. His impact on the congregation was certainly more noticeable. Already older and wiser, he now had some experience behind him, which gave him the confidence to branch out and to try new approaches.

Selwyn and Enid also had personal reasons for viewing their time in West Wales with affection, for it was there, in March 1952, that their first son, David, was born. Soon afterwards, it was time to move on again, for, in 1953, Selwyn accepted an invitation to pastor the Assemblies of God church in South Kirkby, Yorkshire.

South Kirkby, Yorkshire 1953–58

The congregation of his new church was very much the same size as those Selwyn had ministered to in west Wales. Numbers varied between 60 and 70. The problems and the opportunities he faced were also similar to those found in

Llandilo and Pontardulais. A great deal of effort and application would be needed to realise any substantial growth. Once again, evangelism and pastoral care were of crucial importance. Selwyn rose to the challenge, applying himself with characteristic vigour, energy and commitment to the various tasks that confronted him.

Looking back, he sums up the five years at this church as 'glorious'. His preaching flourished, as did his pastoral work. Not long after his arrival, a hundred young people were converted in a crusade. As ever, he was a fervent evangelist, taking very seriously the commission of our Lord to preach the Gospel at every opportunity. At the same time, he was painstaking in his attention to detail – the church must be built on none other than the solid, unshakeable Word of God. Evangelistic, devotional and practical teaching bore fruit – not only in terms of people being converted, but also in terms of their steady personal growth towards maturity and stability. As always, he taught his congregation not only to look their problems in the face, but also to see them in the steady light of Scripture. This is a constantly recurring theme in his ministry, and he would often remind his congregation of the other ingredients vital to Christian growth and maturity. Once they had squared up to their difficulties, Selwyn encouraged every believer to make a daily 'appointment' with God:

Establish a time as soon as possible after you awake, when you can spend time alone with Him in prayer and contemplation. I know of nothing that sharpens the awareness of God's presence in a believer's life more powerfully and effectively than the regular practice of a morning Quiet Time . . . Every Christian must try to have some time alone with God at the beginning of the day – even if it is only a few quiet moments. Savour those moments – they will provide you with a fountain in your heart at which you can slake your thirst throughout the day.[1]

Thus equipped, members of Selwyn's flock were able to take a firm stand, leaving behind their former ways and resisting the temptation to sin. Instead they aspired to the love of God, following his example, in obedience to the New Testament commandment: 'Love one another as I have loved you' (John 13:34).

Looking back

The years in South Kirkby were notable in many respects. Selwyn and Enid were becoming a united couple, and Enid was fully involved with Selwyn's work. They undertook together the work of God – Enid being particularly involved in the Sunday School, where she taught regularly. In 1958, Selwyn completed the eighth year of his ministry. At the ripe age of 30, how did he view this first milestone in his career? More than anything, he was conscious of God's hand, guarding and cajoling him throughout the decade:

> In all the moves and behind all the situations lies the governing and guiding hand of a prevenient God. These circumstances provided for me the challenge and the tuition that I needed to absorb in order to be ready for God's call of destiny when it came. At times, passing through the various phases of my ministry, I felt checked and frustrated and sometimes even chained, but now I see that all the time the Holy Spirit was building into my life the pattern of His divine will and was preparing me for the work that would later fill my life.[2]

He was learning to develop his natural abilities using all the discipline of his character – honesty and integrity played a major part. All too soon he had recognised the pitfalls as well as the joys of his chosen profession. As a result, he quickly learned to apply the teaching of the Bible to real life situations in which people backslid, became confused by the 'slings and arrows' of life, were prone to be put off by the slightest difficulties, were critical in their attitudes, were easily diverted by Satan's temptations. They were in need of a minister who would sympathise with them without condoning their sins and who would, above all, direct them to the plain, unadorned teaching of the Bible. He also began to develop counselling skills which would enable him to help people to the fullest possible extent.

Because Selwyn worked in relative obscurity, with small congregations in far-flung parts of Britain, this allowed him the freedom to develop his own ideas. He was not yet within the gaze of a wider public. Many of the lessons he learned in Helston, Llandilo, Pontardulais and South Kirkby were later to be used in the work of CWR. He learned especially the best ways of communicating the Gospel to others. God was calling him to a very special work and it was perhaps in anticipation of this that, in 1958, he began to feel restless:

Despite the anointing of the Holy Spirit and the evident blessing attending my ministry, I felt a deep dissatisfaction within my heart. I knew that God was preparing me for something else and so sure was I that I should break with denominationalism that I entered into something that almost brought disaster. I resigned my church in South Kirkby in 1958 and moved to Sheffield.[3]

By purely human standards, this would be a foolish move. Was he really right to give up the security and success of his work in Yorkshire? Suddenly, Enid and Selwyn found their equilibrium shaken – life in Sheffield was indeed precarious.

Chapter Four

A TURNING
POINT: 1958

*. . . another way of
looking at things*

Invited by a group of people who wanted to start a new church in Sheffield's city centre and emboldened by the conviction that Sheffield was the place to which God had called him, Selwyn set up a campaign in the City Hall – right in the heart of the bustling city. It seemed ideal for his purpose, which was to introduce Sheffield's entire population (of about half a million) to the Gospel.

However, it was soon evident that the location of the site was not as good as it had at first appeared. Its nearness to the local Assemblies of God church led to a bitter conflict. Selwyn describes this difficult period in his autobiography, *Walking with Destiny*, which was published a few years later. Being an Assemblies of God minister himself, his new venture, which was quite separate from the denomination, was called into question: 'For months I continued to lead the crusade from the City hall against a background of misunderstanding, argument and debate.' Eventually he conceded defeat and closed the crusade, then subsequently resigned from the Assemblies of God. Although his high hopes and aspirations were dashed to the ground, Selwyn really had no alternative but to leave.

Undoubtedly he was not the only one to feel wounded. Those who had raised such strong objections to his campaign may themselves have felt torn apart by the controversy. Feelings on both sides were raw. The severance of his life-long connection with the Assemblies of God was a painful process for Selwyn. Despite the inner turmoil, however, he believed that this was the right course of action. With hindsight, he regrets the arrogance with which he handled the incident. He was perhaps more aggressive than he should have been and realises now that this approach could certainly not have advanced the cause of the Gospel.

Selwyn's home church in Fochriw supported him in his belief that the rule which meant that no Assemblies of God minister could open a church within two miles of an existing one, applied by the Assemblies of God in Sheffield, was ridiculous and legalistic. Today, he has good, cordial relations with the AOG and receives many invitations each year to preach at its churches.

Healing

Following the birth of his second son, John, in May 1958, Selwyn was stricken with a strange illness. For weeks he hovered between life and death. Delirious and weak, with a dangerously high temperature that resisted all attempts to bring it down, he could hardly lift a cup of water to his lips. His condition was diagnosed as double pneumonia, although he was later told that it was, in fact, much more complex. No doubt the traumatic events in Sheffield were a contributory factor to this illness. Whatever the underlying causes, Selwyn was, understandably, stunned and bewildered by the turn of events:

> For several hours after receiving the news that I was soon to die, I tried to put my thoughts in some kind of order. I remember thinking: what will happen to my wife, Enid, and my two young children, David, aged seven, and John, just a few months old? Why should God permit me to depart this life at the age of 30, when my ministry was really only just beginning? Must I resign myself to the situation and accept it as the will of God?[1]

Feeling so unwell, he began to prepare himself for death. In search of comfort, he reached for his Bible, with the intention of turning to John 14, that well-known chapter of comfort, but the book fell open at chapter 10: 'The thief comes only to steal and kill and destroy,' he read, 'I have come that they might have life, and have it to the full.' The words leapt off the page. Selwyn felt them as a physical force: 'An explosion seemed to take place deep within me, and for several minutes my whole body appeared to be flooded with divine power.'

The impact was staggering. Until this point, he had believed that sickness was sent by God – either as a punishment, or as a purifying fire that would burn the blemishes from one's soul. Now he discovered something entirely different! The 'thief', he realised, refers to the devil and it is *he*, not God, who brings ill health. Jesus, on the other hand, comes to bring life!

Selwyn immediately felt the new life of Jesus throbbing through him. He was amazed that such simple words had brought with them such a blinding revelation, overturning many of his former beliefs in one fell swoop. The fact that Jesus is the author of abundant life caused a surge of strength, and he leapt out of bed, perfectly well. Enid was alarmed to find him walking around the bedroom, hands aloft, shouting and praising God:

> My wife who, at that time, was downstairs, bravely trying to cope despite the fact that she knew her husband was dying, came running upstairs and stared at me in amazement. She told me later that, as she had never seen anyone die before, she thought that this was the way Christians always behave just prior to going to glory! 'What's happened?' she said. 'I'm healed,' I replied. 'God just touched me when I was reading John 10:10.' She seemed unable to take it in. Then we both burst into tears. We hugged, we cried, we laughed and we thanked the Lord for the demonstration of his healing power.[2]

As if this was not enough to get excited about, there was another healing soon afterwards. Fearful that any further stress would upset him, Enid had kept from Selwyn, while he was sick, that their younger son, John, was also seriously ill. Now she told him. Selwyn reacted by simply placing his hands on the baby and praying that God would heal him. Within an hour, John had improved dramatically.

Medical opinion would suggest that Selwyn's illness, in particular, had undergone a 'spontaneous remission'; but, nevertheless, he is adamant that he was supernaturally healed. In any case, the event was a turning point for him and launched him into a ministry that he would never have dreamed was possible.

In his pastoral ministry up to this point, Selwyn was reticent whenever anyone asked him to pray for healing: 'Lord, heal this person *if it is your will,*' he would say. Or, 'Teach this person *how to bear this sickness* for your praise and glory.' However, after his own healing, he began to see things in a different light. It was just possible that one could actively resist sickness, and even *fight* it, in the strength of God and the power of the Holy Spirit. So he did three months' intensive study of the Biblical foundations of healing.

Concentrating on the attitude of Jesus towards sickness, Selwyn read through the four Gospels from start to finish. In the process, he discovered 26 cases of individual healings and ten cases of multiple healings. He found that Jesus healed people for three specific reasons. First, as a direct expression of the mind and will of God. Into this category may be placed the man born blind (John 9:4) and the leper (Mark 1:40–41). Secondly, to validate His claim of being the Son of God. In Mark 2:1–12, for example, he records the healing of the paralytic who was brought to Jesus by His friends. Lastly, Jesus healed the sick because of His great compassion. In Matthew 14:14, for instance, 'And Jesus went forth and saw a great multitude, and was moved with compassion toward them, and he healed their sick.'

Selwyn then went on to study the ministry of healing by Jesus' disciples, especially in the book of Acts. Finally, he analysed the epistles, concluding that the ministry of healing should be an integral part of every community of Bible-believing Christians. His background reading complete, he felt full of confidence to step out in faith. He saw God's healing in a completely new light:

> I knew instinctively that no longer would I pray for either my own or someone else's healing with the faith-destroying phrase: 'If it be thy will.' To me, both then and now, the issue is fundamental – for unless God wills healing, then it is useless to pray for it. If we pray with positive words – 'Lord, bring healing to this person in your name' – yet hold a contrary belief in our hearts – 'I wonder do you really want to heal this person, Lord?' – then faith will be

sabotaged by doubt. Although my study of the Word of God still left me with intellectual problems concerning healing, the issue of whether sickness is the will of God was for ever settled. Not once, since the moment I ended my special study of the Scriptures, have I ever changed, or been tempted to change, that view. This is not to say that at times I do not wrestle with difficulties concerning the matter of healing, but the conviction that God does not will sickness is firm and unshakeable.[3]

Changing perspectives: the USA

There was a period of transition for Selwyn in 1958–59. He continued to live in Sheffield while at the same time becoming an itinerant evangelist in Britain. It was a period, too, when he began to adopt a new approach to church life. He started to view it from *outside* a denominational focus. He continued to believe, of course, in the local church, and still does to this day, but he was now able to move around more freely to preach and conduct campaigns.

Towards the end of 1959, he was invited to work in Colchester Elim Church, where a group of ten churches came under the umbrella of the 'Elim Pentecostal Church'. The congregation was around 60–70 and, again, it was a time in which Selwyn grew and developed as a minister and as a counsellor. He was in something of a dilemma, however, because although he saw Colchester as only a temporary stopping place, he was unclear about the direction of his future ministry.

In 1961, he was invited by Rev Harold Groves, a minister from Reading, Pennsylvania, who had heard about Selwyn from a close personal friend, Dr Jack Martz, to go to America. This was the first of many visits to the USA. The trip lasted three months, with his wife and two children staying in England. His first crusade was in Reading itself, where he was given a very warm welcome. From the first service there, Selwyn felt an inner witness in his spirit that God was going to bless him in an outstanding way in America.

The crusade was due to last for eight days, but it went on

A view of Fochriw, Selwyn's home village, taken in the early 1920's. South Tunnel Terrace was off to the left on the hill the picture is taken from. (*County Library, Dowlais*)

Fochriw railway station looking towards Bargoed (early 1920's).
Selwyn daily rode the train there after winning a scholarship to
Bargoed Grammar School in 1940. There was great excitement,
he remembers, among schoolboys at their free rail pass: it was
often used to make evening visits to the town after homework
was finished! *(County Library, Dowlais)*

The Pentecostal church in Fochriw. It was here in February
1944 that Selwyn was converted. Then surrounded by terraced
houses, it now stands alone on the edge of the village. *(Harold
King)*

Sunday School anniversary, South Kirkby, 1955.

Selwyn in Atlanta during his 1961 USA visit, seen here with long-standing pastor friends, Tolbert Moore *(right)* and Gene Winfrey *(left)*.

Saturday afternoon outreach in Trafalgar Square became a regular feature of the London Revival Crusade.

Volunteer helpers packing *Every Day with Jesus* and *Revival* at the Weybridge office.

Selwyn and Enid with sons David (*left*) and John (*right*) at home in East Molesey, Surrey, early 1960's.

Selwyn with overseas delegates at Denison House during a 1968 World convention.

Selwyn with Sam Park at whose invitation Selwyn led a
three-week crusade in Korea in 1968.

Selwyn speaks to crowds of around 30,000 in Korea in 1968.

Pastors' seminar in Triuanrum, India, 1972. Selwyn seen accompanied here *(on his left)* by CWR team member, Eric Bowtell.

Addressing a Holy Land tour group at Jacob's Well, Sychar in 1979.

for three weeks. Selwyn visited the Deep South, where the hospitality he received by far exceeded his expectations – even though he had already heard great things about the warmth of the people there. The services in that part of America were among the most wonderful he had ever experienced. He received so many invitations to churches all over the country that it would have taken him about two years to fulfil them all. There is no doubt that his trip to the States improved his preaching. In the first place, it gave him the chance to preach to bigger congregations than previously and allowed him to put into practice the lessons he had learned during the whole of the previous decade in England. It also brought him into contact with American evangelicals who placed great stress on the presentation of the Gospel to achieve the maximum impact. Today, clarity of presentation is one of the themes that runs clearly through all the work of CWR.

From the Deep South, he flew to Winnipeg, Canada, into sub-zero temperatures. Selwyn held meetings in the famous Calvary Temple Church, Canada's leading Pentecostal church For the first time in his life he saw his name in lights:

The appearance of the church from the outside resembled a cinema with the services advertised in powerful neon lights. The lights flashing off and on outside the church stabbed out these strange words: 'Featuring Selwyn Hughes – tonight – in "Sermons you will remember".' I couldn't help but chuckle.

He then travelled south again, at the invitation of Dr Tolbert Moore, who recalls those days:

Soon I learned that the Elim Church to which he belonged and was an ordained minister was not Baptist. The fact of the matter was, Elim was Pentecostal. I was, and am, Baptist all the way – too late though – I already loved him too much for the difference in doctrine to separate us. We would spend long hours discussing, sometimes disagreeing –but never disagreeable. He was humble, rather shy, very courteous, yet dynamic in the pulpit. He was bold to preach the gospel. The people of our church and other churches around Atlanta soon learned to love him.

On one particular Wednesday evening he preached across town from us. I was at my own church. When he returned home late that evening I asked him, 'How was the service?' He said, 'Wonderful! When I shouted, they shouted back!' Such were the times with Selwyn Hughes.

As the years have passed, he has developed his skill, progressed in his pulpit manner, reached new heights in his spiritual self and cast aside those things which might hinder him in God's service. He has 'laid aside every weight and the sin which doth so easily beset us, and is running with patience the race which is set before him, looking unto Jesus, the author and finisher of our faith' (Hebrews 12:1).

Some of his ways were seen as rather eccentric. He did not, for example, take to Southern-style food and was very difficult to feed! Tolbert Moore remembers another of his idiosyncrasies:

When he wanted to write, he would ask for a 'day of solitude'. He stayed in his pyjamas, quietly in his room. He worked all day writing by hand and then on the typewriter. Little did I know what God was doing in my little Welsh friend's life and what was in store for the ministry which is now CWR.

Enjoying the beauty of all that he saw around him, Selwyn benefited from the new sights seen and the new friends he made on his travels. However, his greatest thrills were in the meetings. He still remembers those days with lots of nostalgia:

One night I was preaching in Georgia to a crowded congregation of 'Southern Baptists' and my subject was 'The Unchanging Christ'. In that sermon, I made a statement that went something like this: 'What He is, He was, and what He was, He is, and what He was and is, He ever will be.' No sooner had I said this than a stout lady from somewhere in the congregation ran up to the platform, picked me up and swung me around and said, 'Brother Hughes, say that again.' So I said it again, and she commanded me to say it just one more time. So I said it one more time to the delight of the huge congregation.

Another time in the same church, I preached on 'The Devil, Dust and Deity', and, during most of the sermon, half the congregation were standing on their feet shouting 'Amens' and 'Hallelujahs' to everything I said. After the formalism and dryness of some British meetings, I revelled in it, it was a joyous change.[5]

A change, perhaps, but would Selwyn want to *remain* in the United States for good? After one of the meetings, he was introduced to a group of Christian businessmen. They had driven over to have a meal with Selwyn and to make him an attractive proposition – to become pastor of a new church with what was then a decent salary of $200 (about £70) a week. Surely the prosperous state of Georgia would be more comfortable a place to live than the cold, grey British Isles? A ranch-style home would be built to Selwyn's own specifications, while Enid and the children would be flown out at their expense. All he had to do was to pick up the telephone (again at their expense) and discuss arrangements for the removal.

Not a man for snap decisions at the best of times, Selwyn was distressed by their demand for an immediate answer. Characteristically, he asked for some time to think and pray. He was in a turmoil. All his life, Selwyn had found it difficult to make ends meet financially. He was raising a family under severe constraints, and the children were sometimes deprived of things that he would have liked them to have. He himself had never known what it was to indulge in a luxury like a new pair of shoes or a new suit. All the time his trust in God was being stretched to the limit.

He had been brought up to believe that a minister *should* be poor and humble, but hadn't his family undergone enough hardships for one lifetime? This decided him. Yes, surely he owed it to Enid, and to David and John, to accept the offer without any further hesitation. Within just a few days they would be on their way to a new life and a new future. He started towards the door. However, at that moment Selwyn heard God's voice speaking to him 'as if He was standing at my side and speaking direct into my ear':

The words trembled along my consciousness and broke with an explosive force into my soul. *I want you in London!* I stood rooted to the spot. There was no mistaking the impact of those words. It was not my subconscious talking to me or the realm of spontaneous thought for the glow that flooded my being in those moments was something I had never experienced before – or since. In the moment of overwhelming quandary His voice had penetrated my heart, and, although I did not understand at the time the deep, deep import of all that those five words meant, I knew I had heard His voice. His instructions had been made clear. I opened the door and sat once again in the living room amongst the men who were awaiting my decision. They saw by my face that the choice had been made for me. They did not even question or try to persuade me when I gave the answer. It came to me in five words. I passed it on in four.

I must go home!

Later that evening, I knelt in my room and, beside my bed, thanked the Lord that he had made His will clearly known. I remembered thinking that no one could escape the will of God. The room was filled with the presence of the Holy Spirit in a wonderful, wonderful way. I felt as if I was *walking with destiny*. I was caught up in a sense of complete abandonment to the divine will of God.[6]

Back home

Selwyn's exhilarating experience in America was in total contrast to the difficult three months Enid and the family had gone through at home. When they met him at the airport on his return, Enid looked weary and lethargic. The strain on her had clearly been great, and he decided that he would not go away again for such a long time. There were other problems. There was, in particular, a real psychological separation between himself and his son, John, who had almost forgotten who Selwyn was. Naturally this was painful for them both, and John remembers the experience to this day.

For his part, Selwyn felt inadequate as a father. He was now convinced of the *absolute* importance of the family: a timely reminder that it is often the people at home who pay the price for success. Enid, herself, didn't complain, her weary appearance said it all. With this new and clearer understanding of his role as a father and a husband, and with the new confidence he had gained in America, Selwyn turned his gaze towards London, where his ministry took on new dimensions.

Chapter Five

THE LONDON REVIVAL CRUSADE

... revival ... a sovereign act of the Holy Spirit

It was May 1961. By now Selwyn had reflected on the American trip and was increasingly convinced of the urgency of the work in London. The city itself had always fascinated him, and, as a child, he spent hours poring over books dealing with all aspects of life in the great capital. Nor did he tire of quoting Wordsworth's famous poem, On Westminster Bridge:

> Earth hath not anything to show more fair,
>   Dull would he be of soul who could pass by,
> A sight so touching in its majesty . . .
>   Ships, towers, domes, theatres and temples lie,
> Open unto the fields and to the sky,
>   All glittering in the morning air,
> The river glideth at its own sweet will,
>   And all this mighty heart is lying still.

Boyhood memories seemed far away, however, as he contemplated the awesome task before him. British society was undergoing a momentous change in the 1960s. The old moral codes, especially sexual behaviour, were being turned upside down. Youth was in revolt.

The churches were being called upon to respond to this revolution. The charismatic movement was beginning to make its presence felt in the denominations, while the house church movement was gathering momentum. Michael Harper and Arthur Wallis, among others, were spreading the message that the gifts of the Spirit are both available and necessary today. Use of these gifts should be recovered, since they would help bring about renewal and revival in the Church, in Britain and worldwide.

Longing for revival

Like the late Dr Martyn Lloyd Jones, Selwyn has always seen revival as a sovereign act of the Holy Spirit – something that cannot be manipulated or artificially manufactured. His concern for revival dates back to his youth in South Wales where the 1904–5 outpouring of the Spirit was still much talked about. Always longing to see revival for himself, he has read widely about it, thinking over the reasons why it sometimes comes and goes so quickly. Those converted during a time of revival very often seem to return, later, to their old ways of living. Why is this? How will the Christian Church deal with future revivals? From this melting pot of thoughts has come Selwyn's determination to prepare the ground, as it were. Through consistent and ardent prayer, plus an awareness of the problems that have beset previous revivals, he aims to equip ordinary Christians so that they may be fully armed against such difficulties. This has become one of the principal goals of CWR – establishing a richness of spiritual reserves and experience in which the seeds of revival will be able to germinate, growing into healthy and fruitful plants.

Back in 1961, Selwyn felt quite overwhelmed by the enormity of the task facing him in London. Yet time has shown him to possess every ability needed to face up to problems, and then to perseveringly work through them. In fact, difficulties spur him into action, providing him with a fierce determination to succeed. When one door shuts, he immediately starts thinking of alternative routes by which to reach his objectives, always holding on to the clear vision of what he wants to achieve. His enthusiasm is infectious – and how desperately we need to be inspired with such vision today. 'Without vision,' as we read in Proverbs 29:18, 'the people perish.'

The great city

So utterly inadequate did Selwyn feel at the task before him in London that he shed tears of longing over it. However, this crushing sense of desolation did not last long. He decided to make a start by spending a day in London. In May 1961, he took an early morning train to London's Liverpool Street station and walked through the city to the Houses of

Parliament. At 6.30 am, the streets were quiet and the trees lining the banks of the River Thames seemed silent and sullen. Shortly afterwards, however, London was pulsating with life as businessmen hurried to work and tourists crowded the pavements.

Selwyn sat quietly amid the bustle of Trafalgar Square, determined to wait there until God had shown him what to do. Above the heads of the crowd, noisy seagulls wheeled in circles, swooping down towards a small boy who held a loaf of bread in his hands. Each time he threw a crumb to the ground, the birds would dive downwards – much to the child's delight.

Another boy crossed the square, selling newspapers. As Selwyn's first priority was to find somewhere to live in the London area, he bought a copy. 'If God wants me in this city,' he thought, 'He will have to find me somewhere to live.' The very instant he got hold of the newspaper, he knew that there was something in it that God particularly wanted him to see. The headlines did not appear to have any particular relevance. Slowly he turned the pages. A modest advertisement caught his eye. It described a small apartment in Surrey, twelve miles by train from London: at one remove from the hurly-burly of the city, but near enough to reach it quickly. The flat was for him. Within a few weeks, negotiations were complete, and Selwyn and his family moved in.

Once he had the family settled, Selwyn was ready to think more clearly about the exact nature of his work. Not wanting to rush into anything, he cancelled all his preaching engagements so that he could simply wait before God for a few months, or however long it might take for him to be perfectly sure of the Lord's direction. Selwyn waited peacefully, in the hope that his heart would be 'drained of all self-reliance' – so that he would 'move just the way He wanted me to go'.

Eventually, circumstances led him to contact an evangelist from the USA, A.C. Valdez, from Milwaukee, Wisconsin, who agreed to help him launch a crusade in London. Held at the Metropolitan Tabernacle in January 1963, the powerful preaching that characterised the event was backed by constant prayer. As a result, many were converted. This was the beginning of the London Revival Crusade.

Vision

While he was setting up the crusade, Selwyn had an unforgettable vision, still vivid to this day. One evening he was sitting on his bed, his Bible lying open beside him at the story of the rich man and Lazarus, which he had just been reading. He was aware of the usual sounds around him: the murmur of voices outside, a dog barking in the distance, traffic moving down the street. Suddenly, in his mind's eye, he saw the sprawling London metropolis as if it were laid out beneath him: church spires, towers, theatres, offices, shops ... All these stretched to the furthest horizon. Arched over the city, running from east to west, was an enormous highway, on massive pillars above the buildings. Smaller lanes fed into the main road, which swept thousands of people out towards the west.

Selwyn found himself among the masses:

> ... walking with the crowds, and as I walked I knew I was in the company of the ungodly for curses and oaths rent the air. On their faces I saw a look of dull unconcern now and again broken by a forced laugh or some kind of simulated gaiety. Then, for some reason, the movement of the crowd slowed down as if there was some obstruction on the road ahead.[1]

He felt himself becoming as impatient as the crowd around him, wondering what had impeded their progress. When he saw the reason for the delay, he was astounded. Surely it was impossible that one man alone could even attempt to stem the flow of so many thousands of people? But yes, a solitary man was pleading with the crowd to turn back:

> In his hand he held a red lantern which he was waving frantically, crying out at the top of his voice ... Go back ... Go back ... Go back. No one seemed to take any notice. As

I passed him I could see the pain in his face, the tears in his eyes as he gave a warning which no one heeded.[2]

The vision ended horribly. Lifted up above the crowd, Selwyn was shown what lay at the end of the road. It ended abruptly in a sheer drop. 'I realised that I was being held over the edge of hell,' he remembers. Yet still the crowds pressed forward towards the edge, pushing, shoving, jostling with one another as they fought to get ahead. At the edge of the cliff, they did not stop. As if blind, they pushed onward. Hundreds upon hundreds were falling at one time, spilling over the edge of eternity into a fathomless hell. He heard them cry out as they fell:

I caught the screams of agony that arose from despairing lips. I heard the curses, the groans, the blasphemy as they cried out in terror. I drew back in horror, but I need not have feared for I was safe in the arms of Jesus – but they? ... they were lost![3]

London Revival Crusade

After this striking vision, Selwyn became more and more occupied with meeting the needs of a lost world. Although he had founded the crusade with revival specifically in mind, he increasingly turned his attention to evangelism. He felt God was showing him that these were to be the joint thrusts of the work in London.

The London Revival Crusade operated from Denison House in Vauxhall Bridge Road, South London. This venue held 400 people and, from 1963 until 1968, a 'Holy Spirit Rally' took place every Saturday night, drawing visitors from all over London and southern England. Hundreds of people were baptised in the Spirit at these gatherings, an experience frowned upon by traditional evangelicals. Although the appearance of spiritual gifts was causing a great stir in the church, Selwyn and his fellow workers were careful not to view the gifts as an end in themselves. Baptism in the Spirit was merely a *preparation*, a powerful force to be channelled into evangelism and, ultimately, revival. Revival remained their long-term goal.

A notable conversion

One man influenced by this outreach was pop singer Terry Dene, who was a teenage idol in 1957–59. His rise to riches and stardom was rapid, as shown in the film, *The Golden Disc*. Originally named Terry Williams, his first major engagement was singing between rounds at the 1957 World Wrestling Championships at the Royal Albert Hall. Spotted there by BBC television producer Jack Good, Terry was signed up for *Six–Five Special*, the top-rated TV pop music show of its day, and for Decca records by Dick Rowe.

His demise was as rapid as his ascent to stardom. A highly publicised relationship with Edna Savage (whom he subsequently married), psychiatric problems and a violent beating up at the hands of thugs all combined to cause his downfall. *The People* newspaper described his story as 'a warning in a crazy teenage world'. However, one wet night in Trafalar Square, he found Jesus Christ. Later he became a street-corner evangelist. Some thirty years after his heyday as one of Britain's first rock'n'rollers, he attempted to make a comeback.

Midnight Express

As well as regular weekly evangelism, Selwyn and his workers were constantly looking for new, even startling, ways of attracting attention to the Gospel. A particularly innovative idea was the publication of the *Midnight Express*, a newspaper describing what the world would be like the morning after Jesus Christ had returned for his people. One million copies were printed and handed out at all major railway and underground stations in London. The impact, if brief, was enormous. Another initiative was the Trafalgar Square rallies on Saturday afternoons. The primary thrust was, again, evangelistic and aimed to take the Good News into the heart of central London.

These years were exciting and invigorating, not only for Selwyn but also for his team of workers. One of them was Vic Ramsey, an evangelist who had first met Selwyn in 1952 in Thurnscoe, Yorkshire, when the two men had struck up a warm friendship. Loose contact was maintained between the two men until, in the 1960s, Selwyn invited Vic to join him in the work of the London Revival Crusade. Vic recalls Selwyn's ministry at that time with some admiration. For example, Selwyn would often simply disappear for days at a time so that he could fast and pray in preparation for his work. He had been impressed by the simple faith of various Americans he had met, who showed him the necessity of *waiting* upon the Lord. This was far more honouring to God, and far more effective, than a half-hour prayer meeting squeezed in between other activities. As a result, meditation and intercessory prayer now became the foundation for all Selwyn's activities.

Vic also remembers a change in the style of Selwyn's preaching at this stage. He was now at his best when coolly and calmly expounding the cardinal doctrines of the Bible. In fact, he would rank Selwyn among the outstanding preachers of this century. His fluency and deep study of the words of Scripture created a ministry that touched Britain and many other parts of the world. Right from the start, Selwyn held firmly to the conviction that only the very best was good enough for God. Inevitably there were problems, too, both financial and emotional but out of it all grew a rich and exciting ministry – the product, in part at least, of Selwyn's tenacity and burning determination to give himself to God's work.

As well as developing his own skill as an evangelist, Selwyn also learned, in the early 1960s, to inspire others who were to work with him. Among them were Gordon White, Tony Holloway, Peter Douglas, Ron Howe and Eric Bowtell, the last mentioned who was later to accompany Selwyn on many overseas trips as a Gospel soloist. His horizons were constantly widening. In 1964, he spent a week in America studying the ministry of David Wilkerson, whose book *The Cross and the Switchblade* became a bestseller in both Britain and the USA. This inspired Selwyn to try to reach London's down-and-outs, particularly those in Soho. He started a meeting for drug addicts, which was held every Sunday night in Orange Street Congregational Church.

Selwyn was now responding boldly to the fundamental changes taking place in the society around him. His love for others and his desire to bring them under the transforming, healing power of the Gospel spurred him on to a constant search for new ways of influencing people. Some of these, like *Midnight Express*, may have been novel and eye-catching, but he has never been one for gimmicks. His whole outreach was rooted in the Word of God, and presented in ways which were relevant to every-day life and its problems. While choosing the most effective forms of presentation, he kept deference to the dignity and holiness of Scripture. He was making an impact on London. Soon he was to spread the message even more widely.

Chapter Six

CRUSADE FOR WORLD REVIVAL

*Man's extremity is
God's opportunity*

From 1963 until 1968, Selwyn continued to run the London Revival Crusade from Denison House. Early in 1965, someone asked him about his method for reading the Bible. He told them that he usually took a Biblical theme and then studied it from different viewpoints. He was asked if he would let others join him in this thematic search of the Scriptures. So Selwyn began sending a postcard each week to 15 people outlining a single theme. The following is an example:

THOUGHT FOR THE WEEK
BE A GOOD SOLDIER FOR CHRIST

A mother heard her young son praying and made this wise suggestion, 'Son, don't bother to give God instruction, just report for duty.'

Theme of the Week:
SEVEN WAYS IN WHICH GOD WORKS FOR US

Sunday
He brings us out
Galatians 1 Memory Text v.4

Monday
He rids us of bondage
John 8 Memory Text v.32 & 36

Tuesday
He redeems us
Titus 2 Memory Text v.14

Wednesday
He makes us into a people
1 Peter 2 Memory Text v.9 & 10

Thursday
He is unto us a Father
2 Corinthians 6 Memory Text v.18

Friday
He brings us into fellowship
John 17 Memory Text v.24

Saturday
He has begotten us into a lively hope
1 Peter 1 Memory Text v.3

At the time, this was a completely new approach to Bible study. Within a few weeks, more than 50 people had asked to join the scheme, and the numbers were continuing to increase rapidly. The cards were printed at Denison House by Harry

Curle, whose wife, Olive, was Selwyn's secretary. Within six months, he was printing hundreds of cards, so a more efficient way of producing the notes was needed to keep pace with the growing demand. *Theme of the Week* became *Theme of the Month* and the postcard became a booklet. These notes were, as Selwyn admits, simplistic, the overall argument being rather thin in content, naive in expression. This was the case with the notes for January 8th 1967:

Daniel 3:13-18
'Our God ... is able to deliver us.'
IS ANYTHING TOO HARD FOR THE LORD? Is it? Do you believe in the fact that He is able to do *anything*. This week, as we look at some of the things He is able to do according to His own Word, you will become convinced of how great and how powerful He really is.

It is when the trial is greatest that it is the most use to God. The greater the difficulty, the more of His power and miracle-working ability is required to solve the difficulty. 'When I had great troubles,' said Frances Havergal, the gifted, sacred poetess, 'I always went to God and was wonderfully carried through; but my little trials I used to try and manage myself, and most often signally failed!' How true this is! If life were full of little troubles alone we should never be called upon to lean completely upon God. When a large trial comes, we turn to Him – and triumph!

These men of God had honoured God. They had committed no crime. Their lives were at stake and there seemed no way out of the difficulty. All they could do was to throw themselves wholly upon God. They did. They openly testified to His ability and put all the responsibility onto Him. And when they threw themselves upon Him, He stepped in and walked by their side – and delivered them.

Selwyn intended that the notes should be used daily and approached with a quiet and prayerful attitude, because 'nothing can be inscribed on a tense mind'. Although a specific text was given for each day, he recommended that it should be read within the context of the whole passage of

Scripture. The daily reading fitted into a wider theme running through the notes and readers were encouraged to bear this in mind from week to week. At this stage, only people in London were getting the notes, but scores of requests for them were coming in from all over the country. This caused Selwyn to think about a better, more appropriate title for them. He sought the advice of his solicitor, Graham Ross-Cornes and together they formed the trust for Crusade for World Revival. Despite criticism that he was setting his sights too high, Selwyn felt that the outreach was destined to become worldwide, and he was right. Enid, typically, was one hundred per-cent behind everything he did, and this softened the accusations that he was being too ambitious.

Crusade for World Revival (CWR) eventually became the vehicle for presenting *Every Day with Jesus* notes. So between 1965 and 1968, Selwyn's work had two main fronts: London Revival Crusade and CWR. These two moved together, complementing and sustaining each other. The notes were only available to people who committed themselves to pray for revival each day. By 1968, so that they could grasp the whole picture taking shape, they were encouraged to share with others thoughts or points that arose during the studies. Talking about things is often helpful in the development of new ideas. Prayer rounded off each day's notes.

Selwyn's CWR ministry was thriving, as was the continuing outreach into Soho. He had also begun to conduct evangelistic crusades in places like Birmingham and Manchester. At this point an event occurred that opened up fresh avenues of ministry and service.

A dramatic happening

Selwyn was relaxing at home one evening in April 1968 when the telephone rang. The call was from abroad. The caller was Sam Park, who was on deputation work in Finland and Switzerland for Voice of China and Asia, the organisation he represented in Korea. He asked to meet Selwyn the following day. Selwyn wrote down the flight number and replaced the telephone. His immediate reaction was one of disbelief, but the next day he did go to Heathrow.

The two men met and went back to Selwyn's flat in East Molesey. At first the atmosphere was awkward because Sam Park refused to speak to Selwyn. In fact, his mouth was covered by an handkerchief. When he removed it, blood poured from his mouth. Only then did he reveal that he was suffering from tuberculosis of the lungs (an illness endemic to Korea). When he contacted a minister in Switzerland, Selwyn's name kept coming to his mind. Convinced that God would heal him, he found Selwyn's telephone number and eventually got through to him. He asked Selwyn to pray, believing, in spite of the blood still pouring from his mouth, that God would heal him.

Selwyn was flabbergasted. He had no faith whatsoever, but Sam kept saying, 'Do it now!' Selwyn still had no faith, so Sam grabbed his wrist, demanding that he pray for him. Selwyn prayed briefly, 'Lord, heal our brother.' Though his prayer seemed utterly faithless, Sam raised his hands, got rather excited, then said simply and without fuss, 'God has healed me.'

He had, too. Selwyn and Enid were both bewildered and remained disbelieving. They were brought back to earth, however, when Sam said he was hungry and asked for bacon and eggs. Sam stayed on for a few days and Selwyn took him to Denison House where his account of what had happened staggered the congregation. The following Monday, he returned to Korea. However, it wasn't the last Selwyn heard of him. Within a week, Sam telephoned again and said, 'Please come at once to Korea.' He wanted Selwyn to conduct a crusade in Pusan, where he was principal of a high school and chairman of an inter-church committee.

Selwyn immediately sensed it was right to accept, although he didn't have the fare to Korea. He prayed for the money and an *Every Day with Jesus* reader in Germany, quite unaware of the need, arranged for money to be transferred to Selwyn's bank account – the exact amount for the flight.

Korea

Selwyn made this trip before Dr Paul Yonggi Cho and Billy Graham made such an impact on Korea. He was met at the airport by Sam Park and given an enthusiastic welcome. He was told that large grounds had been hired and an organisation set up for a three-week crusade. He preached to large crowds of around 30,000 – and thousands were converted.

Selwyn has vivid recollections of one particular prayer meeting. About 5,000 people gathered at 5 am in the local high school to hear Selwyn speak from Acts 10, which tells of the Holy Spirit coming to Cornelius's household. When Selwyn had finished, the Holy Spirit fell in power on the congregation. It is the nearest he has ever come to revival. In the front row of the school hall, he heard quite distinctly a Korean woman speaking in Welsh and saying, 'Diolch iti arglwydd,' which may be translated as, 'Thank You, Lord.'

The Korean trip whetted Selwyn's appetite for overseas campaigns, and it signalled his moving out from pastoral life into the wider ministry of CWR to the world. Between 1969 and 1971, he led crusades in Brazil, Jamaica, Norway, Sweden, Finland, Kenya, India and Denmark. In all of these places, the crowds were huge and thousands came to find new life, forgiveness and acceptance in Jesus Christ.

Financial venture: 1970

Travelling extensively as he did, he was constantly looking for the cheapest way to fly. He joined a charter flight organisation, which arranged flights at very low cost. He then set up his own organisation offering cheap flights to missionaries: Crusade Travel. Again, he was flooded with requests from all over the world. Literally thousands of pounds came in and went out almost immediately. He was advised, by his accountants, to separate CWR from Crusade Travel – advice which he accepted. As a result of dealing with the accountants Neville Russell, David Rivett, now one of the three CWR executive directors, became a CWR trustee.

Dramatic effects of new seminar

In 1972, CWR moved their offices to an old posthouse in Weybridge. Into the new offices one day walked the brother of CWR's artist, Irene Mitcheson. As a result of their conversation concerning a new ministry development in the United States, Selwyn made his way to Atlanta, Georgia, to investigate. He returned having been greatly impressed with the presentational skills of a Bill Gothard, whose communication techniques for teaching the Scriptures regularly attracted congregations of many thousands. Selwyn realised that with a screen and projector he could achieve similar results in Britain, and present the truths of God to people in a fresh and dynamically effective way. He worked out a seminar, *Life in a New Dimension*, later *Dynamic Christian Living* (see Appendix), which proved to be another turning point in the development of CWR.

It was early in 1973 when Selwyn was joined by Alan Richardson as a young assistant. After a time of training and discipling, he worked with Selwyn in presenting the new seminar at venues throughout the British Isles. In all, around 35,000 people would attend.

At the first presentation, Selwyn and Alan led 300 people through the course at London's Westminster Central Hall every night from Monday to Friday and all day Saturday. The impact was quite staggering – especially on the Wednesday evening when participants were taught about gaining a clear conscience.

Selwyn and Alan walked out of the hall afterwards to see people queuing outside the telephone booths. They couldn't wait to contact and apologise to those they had wronged and hurt.

In Glasgow the effect was even greater. Among those attending were a number of students from the Bible Training Institute, including a former jockey. The teaching convinced him that he had to put right an important matter. While riding for a stable at Newmarket, he had been involved in several burglaries and had avoided being caught for the crimes. At the seminar he was advised to see the Principal of BTI, who thought he should go back to Newmarket and confess to the police. Later in court, he explained what had happened to him, and how, through the *Life in a New Dimension* seminar, he had owned up to the offences. The magistrate fined him but was so impressed with his honesty and willingness to make restoration that he paid the fine himself.

A factory worker in another part of the country had been fiddling the accounts. After attending the seminar, he went and confessed to his bosses. The directors heard his case and called him in. Much to his surprise, rather than getting fired, he found himself being offered promotion, so impressed were they with his sense of conscience and integrity!

Life in a New Dimension had two significant effects on Selwyn and on CWR. It was out of this foundational course that CWR's ministry in counselling widened and developed; and it was at one of the seminars in Leicester that Selwyn talked to Trevor Partridge, who began to feel involved with the expanding ministry – a key turning point no less, and the subject of the next chapter.

Chapter Seven

SELWYN
AND
TREVOR

... a man with a servant heart

Selwyn first met Trevor Partridge in 1971. From this sprang the beginnings, in 1973, of a successful partnership, which has continued right up to the present time. From the start Trevor realised the need to be careful of what he calls the 'Absalom principle'. This is the process by which a young man watches the malcontents, possibly to champion their cause. The antidote is a servant heart with regard to people and the whole practice of leadership and authority. Consequently, he regarded Selwyn as the *father* of the work, and never aspired to usurp that role or its attendant status; and he quickly recognised that Selwyn touched people's lives through his own character, personality and work.

Trevor was born in Baseford, Nottingham. Brought up in Loughborough, he was converted to Christ as a young boy, but it did not become a serious commitment until his late teens. He attended the local Pentecostal church but was unhappy there for a number of reasons. There was a split in the church, which caused bruised feelings and antagonism. Trevor also wrestled with a personal struggle and family crisis. His father, a godly man, suffered a prolonged nervous breakdown that disrupted normal family life. Having learned, in church, that Jesus was the answer to all of life's problems, it seemed that those who had proclaimed this so strongly were powerless to help his father. To Trevor, a teenager struggling with his own problems, the Gospel that had been proclaimed did not seem to make sense.

He spent four years studying at Seattle Bible College in the USA. The course was more broadly based than any available in British colleges at that time, and it helped him to study Biblical psychology and pastoral counselling as part of his theology degree. He supported himself during his time in the States, graduating with a theology degree in 1972.

In the early 1970s Trevor was concerned about the excesses of the charismatic movement, preferring to stress, instead, the need for personal responsibility and repentance. In this sense, he is not a traditional charismatic – more a pragmatist, interested in maintaining a steady walk with Christ through the ups and downs of every-day life. He is interested not so much in how high a person may leap in the emotionally charged atmosphere of a meeting, but how steadily they live out their faith in the daily routine of life, work and church.

Close rapport

Secure in his own position, Selwyn was mature enough to give Trevor his head in the organisation of CWR. Recognising Trevor's strengths and abilities, he utilised them to the full so that between them they could achieve the maximum creative potential. Even today they continue to work harmoniously, achieving much more together than they would have done apart. Selwyn provides the inspiration, while Trevor is the driver, the motivator, and remains a preacher at heart. They also have a common vision for a Christian college in Britain, as part of a system of Christian higher education. Their common burden is to establish a training centre which deals theologically with the practical, daily aspects of Christian life and vocation. They have now met this target with the opening of Waverley Abbey House in 1987. When Trevor first came to CWR, it was a far-off dream.

In the early days, Selwyn and Trevor travelled extensively together, sharing all their ideas, thoughts and hopes. Whilst one was doing the driving, the other would make notes on their discussions. They would think out loud as they drove along, bouncing ideas off each other. In this way a close rapport was built up and mutual respect is the key to the success of their partnership. They also hold in common a steadfast determination to loyalty, never descending to personal criticism in front of CWR staff, and this helped to preserve their working relationship when later (and perhaps inevitably) they disagreed quite fundamentally.

In 1973, when Trevor joined CWR, Selwyn had six other employees. The offices were in an old post house in Weybridge: paper peeled off the walls, water seeped in through the leaking roof, and the filing system was, at best, rudimentary. The financial position was precarious, the debt being in the region of £50,000. For the next two years, CWR limped along, and by 1975, urgent and immediate action was needed. Towards the end of the year, the pressure was so intense that Selwyn, Trevor and the other staff got down to some serious prayer. *Why* were they in such a difficult situation? No immediate answer became apparent, but soon Trevor initiated changes relating to *Every Day with Jesus* that brought them into a much healthier position.

Every Day with Jesus: strategic changes

At the end of 1975, 80,000 copies of EDWJ were given out each month free of charge. There was no direct income from them. Then, largely at Trevor's insistence, CWR introduced a major change, requiring its readers to make a *commitment to pray for revival* in return for receiving the notes. The number of copies sent out plummetted to about 12,000. It was subsequently decided to split off the CWR Prayer Chain from *Every Day with Jesus* and *sell* the notes in order to provide some much-needed income. This led to yet a further drop in the number of copies sent out – 8,000 in 1976.

Trevor tried to get the notes into the Christian bookshops, only to find that Scripture Union had cornered the market, as he had suspected. He tried for another two years to get *Every Day with Jesus* accepted and established in the Christian publishing world as a devotional aid to Bible study. These initiatives caused the circulation to grow, and a major new strategy was undertaken. This consisted of putting a free copy into a selection of Christian magazines such as *Crusade, Life of Faith, Family, Renewal* and *Buzz*. The 'loss leaders', distributed in this way, amounted to a quarter of a million copies. Trevor also put the relevant magazines' names on the front of *Every Day with Jesus*. To the publishing world this was an admirable but crazy thing to do, especially as CWR agreed to pick up any losses incurred by the bookshops. The results were not dramatic at first. Within six months, however, the number of copies sold had advanced by something like 50,000, and from that moment the notes have increased in popularity each year. Following this, Kingsway, a Christian publishing company, approached CWR about establishing some form of trade distribution. *Every Day with Jesus* is now one of the success stories of Christian publishing, due, in part, to the dynamic and courageous marketing methods introduced and developed by Trevor. All proceeds from the sales go direct to CWR – neither Selwyn nor Trevor have ever received a royalty from this publication.

Serious disagreements

For ten or so years there were no *major* disagreements between the two men. In 1984, however, communication between them broke down, though not intentionally on either side. Selwyn felt that Trevor was forging ahead to the extent of usurping his control, and this he objected to. They found that they were making decisions quite independently of each other, with no coming together on policy. There were other pressures, too. Selwyn's wife, Enid, became unwell and this was a cause for great concern. Meanwhile, Trevor was fully occupied with the establishment of Waverley Abbey House and wanted to divide the mechanics of publishing from the ministry of lecturing, training and counselling. He proposed that they should both become directors, receiving salaries and working in harness. There was still no communication and matters quickly came to a head. Selwyn felt that they could no longer work together. At this stage, when they were obviously growing apart on a personal level, the whole work and outreach of CWR could have been seriously jeopardised, were it not for one fact: *they both committed themselves to reconciliation.* For both it was a period of pain, confrontation – and, ultimately, repentance. After six months of working through their problems, with David Rivett as an intermediary, their relationship was restored. They then met with the rest of the CWR staff and honestly shared the struggles and differences that they had worked through. The issue was resolved in a mature, sensible and realistic way. Their unity of purpose and intention, once re-established, was a crucial factor in the extension of CWR's work.

Today their relationship is that of equals: Selwyn, Trevor and David Rivett are the three executives of CWR. Selwyn and Trevor also enjoy a close, personal relationship. Perhaps the most well-known fruit of this partnership is *Every Day with Jesus*, the Bible reading notes that are used widely throughout the world.

Chapter Eight

SELWYN THE COMMUNICATOR: EVERY DAY WITH JESUS

. . . you can never exhaust the meaning of the Scriptures

It has been suggested that Selwyn enjoys one of the largest daily congregations in the world through *Every Day with Jesus*. First produced in 1965 as an aid to personal revival, the notes probably go into more homes around the globe than any other comparable publication. For eight years they were sent out free. Then, because the circulation had increased so much, a charge became essential, as explained in the previous chapter. *Every Day with Jesus* is now available on subscription as well as being on sale in Christian bookshops. It is read in at least 126 countries and in 1989 the bi-monthly circulation had reached over 200,000 copies. As well as *Every Day with Jesus* itself, there is *Young People's EDWJ*, also *Through the Bible in One Year*, a study on Bible characters, *The Life of Christ* and many other study guides.

Selwyn has had a life-long interest in communication. As a child he was bored by maths and science but thoroughly enjoyed language (he learned both English and Welsh at school). Fascinated by words, he loved reciting poetry and would read anything he could lay his hands on. As a boy he would sometimes read under the bedclothes at night by torch-light. He has always longed to communicate as effectively as possible and has meticulously applied himself to this. It has not always been easy. His early attempts at writing for a Christian audience were not exactly successful. He wrote an article for *Redemption Tidings*, the Assemblies of God magazine, only to receive a discouraging response from the editor: 'With your tendency to wordiness, you will never make a writer.'

Selwyn's first attempts at writing were wordy indeed. However, he soon learned to be self-critical and developed restraint. Nowadays, he never allows words to run away with him, and is much more concise – something which is reflected in *Every Day with Jesus*. Selwyn always keeps to one typeset page of 300 words for each day's notes and is discriminating in the vocabulary he chooses. Brought up on a diet of fiery preaching, he has an outstanding ability to reach the emotions.

Both verbally and on paper, his sentences are so shaped that they have a forceful impact which seeks a response from his listeners and readers.

Being much-travelled, having met all kinds of people and undergone many trials, Selwyn is able to bring a wealth of experience to EDWJ readers. He uses it creatively to explore new themes and new ideas backed by a wide range of illustrations and varied means of expression. Creativity has become second nature to him.

If *Every Day with Jesus* is well-constructed and stylishly written, the content is of equal quality. There are no flights of fancy – no empty words. Realising that what is *not* said is every bit as important as what *is* said, Selwyn has also identified the value of nailing misconceptions. Profound truths are made clear and simple.

Scripture

Every Day with Jesus, as the title suggests, aims to apply the Bible to the routine experiences of every-day life. Selwyn believes with unswerving confidence that Scripture is the Word of God. Like his first pastor, David Thomas, he would say to everyone: 'Take the Bible by faith.' The classics of Christian literature, however inspired they may be, can never take the place of Scripture. Yet *because* it is different from other books, *because* it is divinely inspired, we need divine help to understand it. 'That is why,' writes Selwyn, 'we must come to it with a prayer on our lips, that we might not only understand it, but know how best to translate its message into our daily lives.'

At the beginning, then, is prayer – a prayerful heart being the prerequisite for all Christian growth. However, prayer is not easy. Selwyn is the first to acknowledge that it is sometimes more a duty than a delight: 'We fall upon our knees and are almost glad when the exercise is over; then we move out to salve our conscience in some active work. But this is where we make a tragic mistake. We cannot really get on with God until we know how to converse with him properly.'

Prayer is a reality. This must be emphasised. When we pray, we 'touch the infinite resources of heaven', which allows us to be transfused with God's power. 'As we converse with the Lord,' Selwyn believes, 'vitality and virtue flow from him to us.' Then things are placed in their proper order and life takes on its true meaning. Prayer is also a release, which prevents us from being too self-centred or gripped by doubt – a dynamic antidote to the cares of the world.

Having encouraged his readers to prepare themselves in prayer, Selwyn then uses *Every Day with Jesus* to teach them about God's Word and its place in their own lives. He sees Scripture as the centre to which we should always return:

> Experience has shown that the best way to begin a Quiet Time is by reading the Scriptures. This is why, now over twenty-two years ago, I began writing *Every Day With Jesus*. Prior to that, whenever I recommended people to begin their Quiet Time by reading the Word of God, they used to say: "But I don't know what to read."
>
> You cannot know the joy it gives me to know that thousands of people who hitherto had no daily Quiet Time now begin their day by reading the Word of God, followed by these devotional thoughts. My words, I know, help many, but they are not one-millionth as powerful and effective as the words of God. For through the Scriptures, Life speaks to life. God has gone into His Word and so, when we read it – God comes out of it.[1]

What, then, should one *do* with Scripture? How does one go about reading it? Selwyn is a great believer in Biblical meditation. By this he means:

> the process by which we take a text, thought or phrase from the Word of God and roll it around in our mind, passing it backward and forward, letting it go out of consciousness, prodding it, absorbing it, admiring it over and over again until its inherent power pervades our whole personality. God has gone into His Word and God has to come out of it. Meditation is the way.[2]

Having once heard, believed and practised the truth, one can then begin to enter into a real understanding of it; and once we understand God's truth we are better able to understand His will for our lives. At every point, we should be checking ourselves against His Word. 'Then and only then,' writes Selwyn, 'are we in a position to specifically seek God's will and guidance regarding any particular issue.'

Practical

One of Selwyn's favourite phrases is that his material 'scratches where people itch'. He has the ability to speak to many different types of people with equal effect. The notes address such problems as fear, loneliness, rejection, suffering and death, temptation, controlling the tongue, alcoholism and sexual temptation. In this extract, for example, he gives a prescription for overcoming frustration:

> Firstly, realise that being a Christian doesn't exempt you from facing problems ... Every Christian is as subject as a non-Christian to the laws governing accidents, sickness and even death ... Secondly, fix in your mind that the Christian answer is along the line of using whatever comes – justice or injustice, pain or pleasure, compliment or criticism.[3]

Selwyn always helps his readers *think through* their difficulties instead of offering platitudes. The notes are realistic: they do not offer unattainable solutions or goals. There is no false triumphalism either. All the advice given is related to the clear, unequivocal teaching of the Bible. It is certainly not a matter of 'lucky dips' into the Word of God. Selwyn emphatically counsels against such practices:

> This practice of opening the Bible at random and receiving the first word one reads as a personal divine message has brought about much harm ... Although God may sometimes use His Word in this way to speak to His children, it must never become a substitute for the close and careful study of the Scriptures.[4]

In his study of the Bible, Selwyn has always been interested in taking theory and putting it into practice. The 'what' and the 'how' of belief are constantly reiterated themes in his writing. He is not overwhelmed by problems but invigorated by them. This requires an exceptionally direct and honest approach. With no holds barred, he exposes the difficulties that many of us may be aware of but are not courageous enough to voice:

> There are many people who go to church regularly and participate in its rituals and ceremonies but who have not experienced a personal conversion . . . It grieves me to say it, but say it I must – only about two-thirds of the congregations that fill our churches know Christ in a real and vital way. The other third needs conversion.[5]

On personal issues, he is equally direct:

> No matter whether you are rich or poor, you will face problems . . . 'A Christian,' said someone, 'is like a tea bag: he's not much good until he has been through some hot water.' Trials, says James . . . come to test our faith. If you could see the *complete* picture of your life, there would be no room for faith. God keeps just enough from you to give your faith an opportunity to soar![6]

Selwyn has a pastoral concern to set people free from their particular prisons. To those snared by nicotine, alcohol or any other stimulant, he warns that they are building an unreal world in which they can only live temporarily. He understands the temptations; he is not callous or unaware of life's pressures. Yet he forcibly makes the point that 'when we profess to be servants of Christ, we must not allow ourselves to become slaves to anything else'. To those already enslaved, he gives the bright hope that, even now, Christ can open the door to complete release and deliverance from everything that binds them.

Open

Selwyn endears himself to his readers by being open about his own feelings and experiences. After several decades of being a Christian, he is still prone, from time to time, to take the way of independence, rather than dependence upon God. Although he longs to follow God's way in everything, he sometimes wants it on his own terms only. This he freely admits:

> What right do I have to tell you what to do if I am not prepared to face the same issues in myself? I may still have struggles with this issue in the future, but I know for sure that, at this moment, my will is more yielded to Him than ever. Perhaps this is the last battle I shall have to fight on this matter, and when I find myself facing situations in the future that are vague and ambiguous without fearing the outcome, I will know the issue has been settled once and for all. I have exposed my heart to you in obedience to the prompting of the Spirit. I need Him as much as you.[7]

Sometimes this hard-hitting approach will touch on some very sore points. He never beats about the bush but will tackle head-on the issue in question. Our all-too casual approach to Scripture is a case in point. There is a disturbing trend to treat Biblical principles as optional rather than obligatory. We all lapse at some time into 'I suppose I shouldn't really be living like this; I had better try to change – if I can'. This is no good. God's way is the way of obedience, *irrespective of whether we feel like it or not.* 'Putting on the new nature,' Selwyn writes, 'requires first putting off the old nature by asserting, with all the conviction possible, that one is going to go God's way.'

In a forthright way, some of the notes chronicle changes in his understanding of faith. Even though his faith has, for many years, been strong and vigorous, it has not always been expressed in love. It has been aggressive and pushy at times. He may have accomplished many things successfully, but perhaps others were hurt in the process. This kind of faith counts for nothing, as Selwyn came to realise:

Then the Lord took me aside and showed me 'a more excellent way'. He said: 'The faith that you have is fine, but it lacks love. Listen to my word . . . "These three remain: faith, hope and love. But the greatest of these is love."' I listened to what the Lord had to say, meditated upon it and came to see that love is the applied edge of faith. As D.L. Moody put it: 'Love is faith in shoes – going out to serve the least, the last and the lost.'[8]

Many other things have become evident as Selwyn has looked back over his life. *Every Day with Jesus* is often a vehicle for his reflections. With hindsight, disasters are often turning points. They may be caused by sin, ignorance or carelessness, but God has the skill to turn even tragedy to triumph, loss to gain – so marvellously does He bring good out of evil. Readers going through painful trials often need to be pointed towards a wider perspective to help them. The thousands of grateful letters Selwyn has received show the continuing value of his gentle reassurance that God knows what they are going through.

And what about fear? Selwyn is no stranger to it. He often uses past experiences to show how fear and anxiety may be overcome. He tells how his mother's presence, when he was a child, would dispel his fear during thunderstorms. Her loving presence made a world of difference, taking him from terror to calmness. When we are conscious that we are *loved*, fear dissolves as readily as the morning mist. God provides us with just such a love. Whenever we are afraid, the Holy Spirit comes, in love, and 'perfect love casts out fear'. We are expected to respond as best we can to His presence:

He dwells in us, not just for the pleasure of inhabiting our beings, but to lead us to victory over all our problems . . . take courage – the Holy Spirit is with you and in you to take you through the fire and bring you out triumphant.[9]

Readers respond warmly to Selwyn's honest and positive style. CWR receives thousands of letters in response to the daily notes *Every Day with Jesus*. In their letters, people have said of the notes that they:

---

* Encourage
* Contain practical teaching
* Help people in crisis situations
* Speak personally to people
* Meet needs, spiritual, emotional and psychological
* Lead to a release of God's healing power
* Influence the devotional lives of Christians all over the world
* Bring about changes for the better in attitudes and behaviour
* Illuminate the Word of God
* Help ministers/clergy with the preparations of their sermons
* Enable men and women to cope with changes in their lives
* Offer a positive perspective
* Bring people to know Jesus Christ
* Impart comfort
* Are real and honest
* Challenge people
* Are written in a simple, unpretentious style
* Increase understanding of the Bible and the ways of God
* Give hope

The letters range from brief notes like this one:

Thank you, Selwyn, for helping me to understand God as my Father, and also helping me to understand myself. From a broken person four years ago to a person who has received an abundance of God's love, and who is being healed emotionally day by day. Thank you for wisdom through EDWJ and helping me to 'get it together'.

to letters running to many pages, often deeply personal, some of them full of heartbreak and pathos. They speak for themselves:

Today's reading (26th March) on bereavement prompted me to write to you. In 1981, I lost a lovely daughter aged 20

---

years with cancer in her face. She was due to be married the year she died. She first became ill in 1979 and went through the most terrible operations the last one of which removed half of her face. My daughter and I were not Christians and had never ever believed, but through the desperate times we found ourselves praying to God for strength, and I must say we were both given tremendous strength and courage over the months. I know I began to really trust Jesus, but I told Him that if ever anything happened to my daughter, I would never ever forgive Him.

On one visit to the hospital I was told that Jayne had only weeks to live. My reaction was hate for God, hate because He had let me down, I called Him the most awful names I could think of, I shook my fist at Him and told Him that I would never trust Him or bother with Him again. I felt I wanted to die. I cried until I was exhausted.

We brought Jayne home and I found myself in a desperate, frightening situation facing the death of a loved one. One day I fell on my knees and asked Jesus to forgive me because I knew that both Jayne and I could not face these weeks to come alone. On March 7th 1981, my daughter and I both gave our lives to Jesus and she died on 22nd March.

Selwyn, I couldn't have faced all the heartbreak without Jesus, I am 46 years old and have only known Jesus for 6 years and what a wonderful 6 years it has been, I have been baptised in the Holy Spirit, given the gift of tongues, and the gift of writing poems (religious). Jesus is the best friend I have ever had or could ever wish for and am full of joy because I know Jesus loves me. Also my dear daughter is safe in Heaven with Jesus. I feel such a love for Jesus and I know that I shall always love Him and serve Him. I couldn't face life without our Lord now.

Thank you for taking time to read my letter, may God bless you and keep you in His tender loving care.

This extract relates to the November/December 1984 issue of EDWJ:

I am so grateful for this issue of EDWJ as my son had a breakdown in the Spring. This autumn, on the same day, my employer died of a heart attack in the morning and my son took his own life with a shotgun in the afternoon. Tuesday's EDWJ 20th November was a great comfort and I bless you for it. I can't stop the tears but am resolved to battle on in spiritual warfare even more in prayer.

A missionary, with the Overseas Missionary Fellowship in the Philippines, writes:

I've been reading EDWJ for twenty years and I should think that you, through these notes, have been more influential in moulding my Christian thinking and understanding than any one single factor – humanly speaking I mean. I think it's the fact that what you have taught and shared has been daily, continuous, consecutive, and of many years duration that has caused it to have such an influence.

The notes meet *particular* needs on *particular* days. Literally scores of letters could be cited to illustrate this point, but here are just four. The first relates to a tragic happening:

It is almost a year since my husband was killed by a car. It happened late at night and I had to spend the rest of the night in an hotel bedroom. I took out *Every Day with Jesus* and it was as if it had been written for me that day. The date was September 28th 1985.

The second relates to a not unusual marital problem:

I felt I had to write to tell you how much your notes for April 1st 1989 meant to me. You spoke of unjust criticism and the hurt it can cause. That day was our fifteenth wedding anniversary and the previous day there had been an incident at work which had disturbed and hurt me. I did not want my mood to carry over and spoil the day for us and I had lain awake praying about it. I knew that I had a choice in my response – that of the sinful nature or that of the Spirit.

Your notes spoke straight to my heart when I read them

in the morning: that feeling hurt is not wrong, but how we react to it. It was a real blessing to me and I thank you for being willing to share yourself with us.

The third one from a woman troubled by dependence on stimulants:

Reading my daily page from *Every Day with Jesus* and the Scriptures, you asked 'where is your dependency . . . in stimulants or in the Saviour?' I looked at the tablets I was about to take, and trusted the Lord to break this habit. Praise God, I have not had them since that day.

The date she referred to was 3rd December 1987, while her letter was dated 8th January 1988.

Lastly, this is an extract from an American minister's letter (19th September 1987) who had discovered EDWJ while serving with the American navy in Scotland between 1982 and 1984:

Your reading for this past Monday 14th Sept., came so close to our present situation in the congregation where I have been pastor for 15 months, that I had to write to you and tell you how it hit me right between the eyes. You were speaking of how God reveals His purpose, but then often reverses what He has promised to build, and then if we persist He restores beyond what we can ask or think. In our parish, there has been a dearth of Biblical teaching and preaching for a number of years, and the Lord brought me here with several specific promises that He would give us a rewarding and prosperous ministry here. The people and I are expecting much, but yet the decline in numbers continues with the loss of three spiritually perceptive members in the first year, through transfers, and by the similar move of our staunchest supporter and most mature and able member this last month. There are a few hopeful signs, and the Lord's word to me has been to wait and to persevere.

Selwyn is a deeply meditative man, with a strong consistent prayer life. He immerses himself in the Word of God and seeks to follow the Holy Spirit's leading in his writing. This makes him alert to the needs of his readers. Denominational labels don't matter: 'I refuse to wear any label other than that of a child of the living God.'

He has sharpened his focus over the past 25 years and he has mastered the thematic approach to Scripture. His gentle humour lightens the pages and makes them a pleasure to read. He has channelled into the pages of *Every Day with Jesus* the fruits of all that he has learned – especially, perhaps, during the traumatic period of Enid's illness. As well as all this, Trevor Partridge's Further Study section at the foot of each day's reading encourages readers to carry on stimulating their little grey cells.

Chapter Nine

ENID AND THE FAMILY

*'In this place I
will give peace'*

It was on 10th April 1981 that Selwyn and Enid celebrated 30 years of marriage. Throughout all this time, she had been his keenest and most ardent supporter, actively encouraging him in all his activities. Whether preaching, lecturing, counselling or writing, he knew that he could rely on her absolute support, love and loyalty. Her confidence in him was total, reflecting her deep love.

Life was not always easy for them. During their courtship and the early days of marriage in Cornwall, they had very little money and looked on buying clothes as luxuries. Nor was food plentiful, apart from the left-overs Enid was able to bring home from the Culdrose Navy base. This was followed by a series of ministries in quite small churches, which, again, meant low salaries and no spare cash. In 1958, Selwyn got embroiled in controversy in Sheffield which precipitated a serious illness and, eventually, his departure from the denomination he had been a part of all his life. Then, of course, the beginnings of CWR with the many demands made on Selwyn's time and energies – emotional, spiritual and psychological. Through all this Enid gave him her fullest possible support, as well as bringing up the two boys. It can't have been easy for her with a husband who was often away from home, and had schedules and deadlines to keep with hardly a let-up. Enid's involvement – both at home and in his work – meant a busy, even hectic life for her. Together as they celebrated three decades of married life, they could look back with gratitude for the way God had led them and given them the strength to deal with considerable difficulties. They were grateful, too, for His love in the shaping of their understanding of the Christian faith. At that point, they could have been forgiven for looking forward to their fortieth wedding anniversary, which wasn't to be because within five years Enid was dead.

Those five years of her life were marked by a considerable enforced slowing down – which caused her great frustration. The change in lifestyle came through increasing ill-health.

Enid was never brimming with health even as a young woman. She was troubled by anaemia which led to low energy levels and difficulties with eating food. In the early 1980s, her physical problems started to become more acute. In 1982, doctors diagnosed Symmond's Disease, a particularly debilitating illness characterised by an extreme lack of energy. She fought against it with great courage and continued to work at CWR's offices, where she was a mother figure to the rest of the staff.

Enid's self-will and determination were apparent to all who met her, especially those close to her. One distressing feature of Symmond's Disease is that it affects the appearance and leads to premature ageing. Enid looked ten years older than her actual age. For about three years, she went to Guildford to see Professor Marks, an expert in the treatment of the disease. However, by 1985, she began to fail to keep food down – an associated symptom of the disease – so she was referred to a doctor at the Middlesex Hospital. She stayed in that hospital for about two months and was, inevitably, referred to as 'Mrs Every Day with Jesus'. Many investigative tests were carried out, including one for an ulcer, which proved to be negative.

Enid's journal

Early in 1985 Edward England, editor of *Renewal*, suggested that Enid should keep a journal describing her thoughts and feelings about her illness. His intention was that it would eventually be published but it never was. She did make a start on the project. It runs to almost 20 hand-written sides of an exercise book and contains about 3,000 words.

This brief journal is not depressing – as is often the case with the writing of severely ill people – because her attitude, which runs right through it, is one of thankfulness and gratitude to God. Her love for Selwyn also radiates through the pain and discomfort she was so obviously feeling. Her weakness did not prevent her from being grateful to God and to her husband. The journal begins frankly and honestly:

One of the greatest hurdles was to accept my illness because Selwyn and I believed we had a work to do for the Lord, and, most of all, that the Lord would heal me, and keep me fit to do what I truly believed was my duty for Him; and, what with Selwyn's ministry and teaching, how could I accept (and we accept) or even tell Selwyn just how ill I was, and, at times, felt as though I would never see 'tomorrow'. Worse still, how would the two boys accept this when they knew how we both believed.

When I first was not well, we thought it was the usual anaemia, but, as the symptoms persisted, we sought help through our doctor, who also thought anaemia was the problem; but I was getting thinner and thinner and more irritable and ill. All our office staff were praying for me, and, at times, I'm sure they thought it was my last day in the office, and, often unknown to me, as I left for home, they would stop work to pray for me and hold me up before the Lord: what a lovely family, and how I praise God for them.

Typically Enid's primary concern was not for herself:

My main concern was that I must not at any time stand in the way of Selwyn's ministry for our Lord. How wrong I was not to share all my knowledge of the illness I had with Selwyn. This caused him concern. We just had to find out what it was that had so affected my life. Who could I talk to, I didn't want to hinder Selwyn's work. All the time, this was my concern.

Many hours I agonized before the Lord asking, 'Why, Lord, why, what is it? Please take me home so that I would not hinder your work that you have set for Selwyn.' So many times, as ministers' wives, we are expected to be so different. I just want to help some of us. As I got thinner and thinner, I cried before the Lord to show me what I could tell my children.

Other aspects of her illness troubled her too:

Selwyn leading a Caring seminar at Westminster Central Hall, 1986 (*Mick Rock*).

Lecturing at a CWR seminar.

Selwyn and Enid on their thirtieth wedding anniversary, 10th April, 1981.

Selwyn with Trevor Partridge at Waverley Abbey House soon after its purchase, 1984. (*Mick Rock*)

Renovations at Waverley, 1985 (*Mick Rock*).

Lord Tonypandy opens Waverley Abbey House, 29th August, 1987. From left to right: Gilbert Kirby, David Rivett, Lady Anson, (Mayor of Waverley), Lord Tonypandy, Selwyn and Trevor. (*Clifford Shirley*)

Waverley Abbey House today. *(Nigel James)*

Selwyn with interpreter Pratap Singh during a visit to Madras, India, April 1990.

Cake cutting at a CWR twenty-fifth anniversary celebration at
Waverley Abbey House, July 1990. *(Nigel James)*

Still I felt that I could not tell Selwyn how I really felt, and all the doctors told me how lonely I was. Could I tell our staff, no, but should I tell Selwyn, but, more and more, I felt the need to share, but guilty at having to. After years and many visits, Selwyn came to Professor Marks, and we were told what it was, and I shared at last with Selwyn my feelings about his ministry and all the times I'd made him promise not to stop ministry appointments and seminars because of me and my condition, which he must have found difficult.

But I know the Lord won't let anything happen to me while he is away. I do feel that I must get onto paper something that might help other ladies in the same position. I feel that the Lord has allowed this to happen to me for a reason we won't know about till we meet Him.

In fact, Enid found it extremely difficult to accept herself as she was:

I now have an anginal problem which I told Selwyn about straight away. Having told my family, I now had the greatest test to accept myself as I am: the Lord must at times have despaired of me. I could not accept that I was me in spite of my health. I could not earn my acceptance, I must just take it, as the Lord has since shown me. I must take it easy, work for Him still, but in the office a short time. He has sent us a lovely and caring staff. I can't tell how important it is to know that people care and love you although you think yourself unlovable, when you look so terrible. Appearances still count no matter how old you are, and this disease's symptom is premature ageing, but Selwyn didn't seem to notice. I thought how awful I looked, but he loved me for me, not for how I looked – how much easier it was for me when I accepted that.

She continued to be troubled by the fact that she wasn't healed:

How could I testify to Jesus' love and healing power when I was like this – what could I say? 'I love the Lord, He is able to heal, but not me.' This was a real block for me, how could I tell anyone about Jesus' love when I was like this? But what a lesson I was learning. Selwyn loved me, my children loved me, but I couldn't love me, as I was. Again and again, I was stuck with no one to share this with.

Later she did come to accept herself:

I had to accept that the Lord didn't need me to do all the work, he'd sent others to help and take this work on. Secondly, Selwyn was able to help me in the house and go with me on my weekly shopping.

I feel my experience has made me more able to help people in a similar situation. I trust through it all the Lord will show through . . . He will give me the strength . . . I just praise the Lord for Selwyn: he has been so strong and wonderful with me through it all. I am so thankful that he is strong enough to continue his ministry through it all.

Gradually, too, Enid came to a place of real inner confidence and inner security:

I had to come to the end of myself and let Him take over.

Fittingly, the journal ends on a humorous note:

I was in Professor Marks' investigation unit for tests when he asked me via one of his registrars if I'd give him some blood for research, as my stomach condition was very unusual.

I was so amazed and happy that at last here was a man who actually wanted my blood. Of course, I agreed – he thought I was going to say 'no', but I said, 'You've made my day. Take as much as you like, it's nice to know somebody wants it!'

Enid's journal is a poignant document. It is serious but far from morbid. It is introspective but far from cripplingly so. Several themes run through it, including her love for Selwyn, his caring concern for her, the importance of the family, especially the grandchildren, to her, and the goodness of God.

Her belief in Jesus' healing power never wavered, but she would have been less than human had she not wondered why she remained unhealed. She agreed to write the journal because she wanted to help other women facing a similar situation to herself. She also had a special burden for ministers' wives facing similar perplexities. Halfway through the journal, she seems to forget herself and turns directly to address such women: 'Again and again, I was stuck with no one to share this with, *so my main concern is for you, maybe this will help.*' She doesn't minimise her problems, neither does she ignore them, honestly recognising her frustration, even to the extent of admitting her sense of bewilderment. Not once, however, does she fall into self-pity or disappointment with God about her continuing ill-health. What clearly emerges from this journal is the need to be frank with God. There's no point in pretending, admitting openly to Him injured feelings and unfulfilled hopes but with out sacrificing faith or confidence in His love and compassionate care for individuals. Ultimately, it's an encouraging document emphasising, as it does, the best of human love (her husband's) and the best of divine love (her heavenly Father's).

Selwyn's predicament

It was only to be expected that Selwyn should have found Enid's continuing ill-health a difficult problem to come to terms with. One reason was that they were so happily married. Another was that they both believed firmly and passionately in Jesus' ability to heal, yet Enid's condition got worse instead of better. For someone who wrote a book called *God Wants You Whole*, and who was also a public figure, the predicament hardly needs emphasising.

A report in the Southampton *Evening Echo* of the day-long Caring seminar held in the city in November 1985 poignantly underlines the dilemma Selwyn faced:

ANGUISH OF A CHRISTIAN

The Revd. Selwyn Hughes is known worldwide as the head of a major evangelistic group, the author of Bible notes read daily by thousands, and a counsellor of undoubted skill. But he is fighting to come to terms with the fact that his wife has cancer.

A devout Christian, he believes God can and does heal people. So he has prayed and fasted and prayed . . . and his wife still has cancer.

Selwyn Hughes stunned the 350 people packed into the conference, simply called 'Caring', by speaking of his emotional and spiritual anguish over his wife.

Up to this point, his audience – mostly Christians of different denominations – had been busy taking notes, turning up Bible references, chuckling at his jokes.

But the huge banked lecture theatre went totally still as Mr Hughes confessed: 'I'm opening myself to you. Some of you will be disappointed in what you see as a lack of faith. But I'm hurting inside, and if you reject me now, you'll hurt me even more.'

Fellow Christians have hurt him, he said, by bullying him about the promises of the Bible regarding healing. He was not despondent, he said, and was working through this crisis trying to understand. He confronted his audience with the pain suffered by him and his wife to show that under the veneer, people aren't always what they seem.

'We're afraid to be seen as we are, afraid that, if we show ourselves, people won't like what they see.'

1985–86

Cancer had been diagnosed earlier in 1985. That April, Enid was operated on for a partial gastrectomy at St Thomas' Hospital. She and Selwyn celebrated their wedding anniversary in hospital. Afterwards her doctors said that they had removed all the cancer, but her life expectancy was uncertain. She recovered sufficiently by July 1985, however, to fly to Bermuda and America, but when she returned to England she was unable to work at all.

In April 1986, medical tests revealed cancer in her liver. Although Selwyn was encouraged to take Enid to a hospice for the terminally ill, he refused to do so, and kept her at home, caring for her himself. Less than three months later, on Monday 4th August 1986, Enid died at home, surrounded by Selwyn, his mother and sister.

Funeral service and bereavement

Enid's funeral service was held on 7th August 1986 at Walton Baptist Church. After the hymn 'When peace like a river attendeth my soul' was sung, Vic Ramsey (Selwyn's fellow-worker in the London Revival Crusade, twenty years earlier) led the congregation in prayer. Trevor Partridge read from the Scriptures and also gave the address. Saying that he had known Enid for twelve years, during which time he had looked on her as a mother, he went on to highlight some of the outstanding characteristics and hallmarks of her life. He referred in particular to her:

Christian faith:

She was born in Helston, Cornwall, where, as a teenager, her faith was born. She committed her life to Christ, having repented and experienced the forgiveness and love of God. This was the bedrock of her life; it not only motivated her life but sustained her during the years of illness. She brought to life a great sense of peace whenever she was visited. The text seen over the home fireplace, Haggai 2:9, was the reality of her life – 'In this place I will give peace, saith the Lord of Hosts.' This peace came from the security of a spiritual relationship, a peace that drew her to others.

Servant heart

In 1950, when Selwyn came to that small Cornish church, they met and fell in love. They married in 1951 and her life underwent a great change. Now she was the wife of a minister, being fully involved in Christian service, church life, and later as the mother of David and John. She was not a public person, rarely being seen behind the pulpit or on the platform. Her place was not in front of the crowds or in the limelight. She delighted in seeing Selwyn fulfil his place. She did, though, have the ability to relate on a personal level to many people, to get alongside and help them. Inevitably her devotion to his ministry meant sacrifices, and for years they struggled on in small churches. In the mid-sixties, too, when he left pastoral work to found CWR, she, again, had to make sacrifices, but was willing to do so. There was no salary, no permanent home, but she stepped out with a sacrificial spirit into the most insecure of conditions.

I know Selwyn would attribute much of his success and the thriving work of CWR to the years of sacrifice, dedicated support and encouragement of his devoted wife. She continued to support him to the end of her life, and even in the years of illness and pain. For the thirty-five years of their married life, she stood with Selwyn: together they served.

Concern for others:

She had a warm and friendly disposition, always with a cheerful smile, wanting to know how people were feeling. She showed a genuine interest and concern about the needs of others. For many years, she served in CWR's offices and was a mother to the young girls. She gave thoughtful and caring Christmas presents; she delighted in giving meaningfully. She expressed her Christian faith in a quiet and caring, concerned way. She exhibited the character of the love of Christ.

Uncompromising spirit:

During her illness she never complained. When you left her after a visit you felt she had cheered you up. Enid was a living testimony to God's grace. Her faith sustained her, and she had no fear of death.

We shall remember Enid (Trevor concluded) for her devout faith, her great concern for others, her years of dedicated Christian service, and her testimony to the grace of God.

We pay tribute to this beloved wife and mother, and give thanks for her significant life. Her favourite book was the Bible; her second favourite book was that of her favourite author; and her second favourite writer was Helen Steiner Rice.

Today, Enid is no longer with us in the body. She is with her Lord. We rejoice for her, for she has gone to her reward.

Enid's funeral service was, in many respects, a happy occasion. The debilitating years of pain and illness were over, and Trevor guided the congregation to concentrate not on the last years of limited activity but on the dominating aspects of her life and work. It is not an exaggeration to say that, without Enid, Selwyn would not have been able to achieve as much as he has. Her part was much more sacrificial in that sense, and Trevor rightly drew the attention of the congregation to this fact. Her example is not obliterated by her death. Winsome Christian love is, after all, the greatest of a Christian's attributes. This service was followed by a short committal service at Randalls Park crematorium, at which Trevor officiated, assisted by Vic Ramsey.

Selwyn had prepared himself for the trauma of bereavement, but he could hardly have anticipated the extent to which he was 'engulfed', as he put it, by the shock waves of bereavement. He felt, not unsurprisingly, thoroughly disorientated. The day after Enid's cremation, he took his car to the garage to fill up with petrol but couldn't figure out, for at least five minutes, how to do it.

Disorientated he may have been, yet he was still confronted with deadlines. One task to complete was EDWJ for March/April 1987. As he sat at the word processor nothing came, apart from the tears which streamed down his face. However, he was ready to face his emotions, to feel them, and to allow them to affect him. Those emotions did not overwhelm him – rather, he was enriched by them. He talked himself into the need to concentrate, reminding himself of the great truths of Scripture, and was determined to fulfil his many commitments. So he began writing on the theme for that edition, *The Indispensability of Christ*. He had been writing for three weeks when a telephone call told him that his father had died very suddenly on a bus going from Bargoed to Pontlottyn. Listed among John Wyndham's effects in the hospital was 'one copy of Every Day with Jesus'. Selwyn, still numb after Enid's recent death, wasn't affected in the way he might have been. There were no tears. A week later he came to write the notes for 22nd March 1987:

In our examination of the areas of life in which there can be no safe and satisfying substitute for Jesus, we arrive today at the issue of death and bereavement. Sooner or later, everyone has to grapple with the fact of death – it is the common experience of the human race. Whether it is the thought of one's own exit from this world or the loss of a loved one, we cannot avoid the fact. Many writers, philosophers and poets claim that the greatest of all fears is the fear of one's own death. And a lot of people fail to live their lives effectively because of this fear.

What consolation has current thought to give to such people? Here is a sample from a non-Christian who tries to offer comfort to a friend who has written to him about being afraid to die: 'The only immortality we should aspire to is that which is offered to us in the memory of our friends.' He then quoted some lines of George Eliot:

'O may I join the choir invisible
Of those immortal dead who live again
In minds made better by their presence.'

Is this all the world has to offer those who are gripped by the fear of death? Survival in the hearts and minds of those they have left behind? I'm afraid it is. It is, of course, gratifying to think that one can live on in the thoughts and lives of those to whom we have been a good influence, but there is a far richer consolation offered to those who truly know Christ. His offer of life after death is founded, not just on a belief but on a demonstration – the resurrection of Jesus from the dead.

Three days later, under the heading 'What a Comforter', he wrote movingly with an assurance and an opaque honesty:

Over the years I have often given advice to those who have been bereaved; now I have had an opportunity to test that advice in my own life. And what is my conclusion? It works – oh, how it works! On the evening of the day my wife died, I picked up an old copy of *Every Day with Jesus* in which I had written a section on the subject of bereavement. I read: 'Make up your mind that grief is bound to come to you, and when it comes, be prepared and willing to feel it – really feel it. Don't dodge it, sidestep it or repress it. Let it sweep over you. Remember, when you are prepared to face a feeling and not run away from it, really feel it, then you are in charge of it, and it is not in charge of you.' I responded to my own advice, went down into the feeling and found there the sweet comfort of Christ assuaging the pain and softening the hurt. It hurt – but not half as much as it would if He had not been there.

I feel deeply sorry for those who lose a loved one and do not know the comforting presence of Jesus. It is this that helps shorten the period of readjustment. Now I can testify, not just from a theoretical base but from an experiential one – there is no substitute for Jesus in the hour of bereavement.

He went on to consider the various alternative comforts to Jesus Christ, including alcohol, nature, art, literature, and concluded:

There is just no substitute for Jesus in bringing comfort to a person who has been bereaved. During the weeks which followed my wife's call to be with the Lord, I received a huge quantity of letters of condolence. One theme ran through them all: 'God will use your pain and transform it to make your character and ministry more fruitful.' One particular letter moved me deeply. It said: 'One can see farther through a tear than through a telescope.' How beautiful! As I read it, I remembered the words of William Alexander Percy:

'I heard a bird at break of day
Sing from the autumn trees
A song so mystical and calm,
    So full of certainties.
No man, I think, could listen long
    Except upon his knees.
Yet this was but a simple bird
    Alone, among the trees.'

God has wonderfully used the words I have written in *Every Day with Jesus* since the first edition over 21 years ago. The theme which has dominated my writings and the one which I keep coming back to, time and time again, is the truth that everything that happens to us can be used. I am asking God, as I write, that out of my own personal sorrow, God will help me set my grief to music and sing 'a song so mystical and calm, so full of certainties'. If you are called to face bereavement in the days that lie ahead, then remember that our Lord gives grace, not only to comfort, but to increase our contribution. He gives most when most is taken away.

Alongside Selwyn's belief, that there is no substitute for Jesus in bringing comfort, must be placed this conviction:

The few days I spent in Switzerland following my wife's funeral did much to soothe my aching heart. It was a delightful supplement, but it could never be a substitute for the grace and presence of the Lord Jesus Christ. I must emphasise this: there is just no substitute for Him. Supplements, yes. Art, nature, literature – all these can help. But only Jesus can heal.

Written at such a time of personal grief and sadness, those notes had a more than usual impact on readers of EDWJ. A lady from Cheltenham wrote:

I just want to convey my grateful thanks for your section in Every Day with Jesus dealing with bereavement and death. God spoke to me, my family and other relatives and friends very clearly and wonderfully through your comments and the readings from the Bible.

I only purchased the notes on Friday, 20th March, coming in halfway through, and, in fact, my husband started reading them on Sunday, 22nd March – the very day we were told by the doctor that my dear mother-in-law was dying (most unexpectedly) . . . The following days were just transformed by the knowledge that God was speaking to us, comforting us and strengthening us.

Another lady from Hampshire commented:

I refer particularly to the section in which you have dealt with bereavement, for the Lord called my husband home in October last year with cancer, and I now have to bring up our three boys on my own, not alone for the Lord is still with me.

To read your words have helped me a great deal because they have been written by someone who has gone through the same experience as myself, and knows just what it is like to suffer the loss of a loved one.

Yet another woman's letter confirms the healing effect of Selwyn's notes on bereavement:

I felt I had to write to you, to thank you for all the help you have given me through the words of Every Day with Jesus. I've seen new aspects, felt released of burdens, experienced fresh delight, but this month when I read of your wife, I felt I could share your sadness. You see, my dad died six months ago, and I've never felt such an ache or such a loss. Your words of comfort, using your sadness to preach Jesus as an answer to *all* our needs, has reached me because I know you understand.

Looking back

It is clear in retrospect that having to go back to work soon after Enid's death was a blessing and a comfort to Selwyn – 'the dark night of the soul' was no less pressing because of this, but it meant that he had to deal with his grief in a constructive way, even using it to speak more effectively to his readers. Out of the crucible of his own anguish he was able to touch people at deep emotional, psychological and spiritual levels. This is confirmed over and over again in letters sent to CWR.

It wasn't only EDWJ that claimed Selwyn's attention. There was also the refurbishing and redecoration going on at Waverley Abbey House, and important developments in CWR's ministry.

Chapter Ten

EXPANSION AND WAVERLEY ABBEY HOUSE

. . . a jewel in the crown of evangelical Christianity

Selwyn and Trevor had long dreamed of setting up a college that could provide specialist education not available at more conventional Bible colleges, covering in-depth such subjects as counselling and leadership skills. Over the years, this vision has developed and, between 1973 and 1987, CWR began running various courses at places such as Fairmile Court (Cobham), The Hayes Conference Centre (Swanwick) and Pilgrim Hall (Sussex). However, the idea of establishing a permanent training college became increasingly attractive. One day, perhaps, this might even become a Christian university.

In 1982, a reader of *Every Day with Jesus* wrote to Selwyn suggesting that he should take a look at an old house which had recently become available for purchase on the open market: Waverley Abbey House near Farnham in Surrey, some 40 miles south of London. Several weeks elapsed but Selwyn did nothing. Then he got a second letter about Waverley. Spurred into action by this persistence, Selwyn drove over to Farnham. As he walked around the grounds, Selwyn felt strongly that the house would provide a suitable base for CWR's operations. Then Selwyn and Trevor inspected the property together. There was one complication: the building was already on offer to another prospective buyer. The prospects looked dismal. Three months later, however, the contract for the sale had still not been finalised. Selwyn discovered that the owner of the house had gone into hospital. Soon afterwards, he died of cancer. The executors considered three offers for the building – including CWR's of £325,000, which was not the highest. Selwyn and Trevor looked for an indication from God confirming the rightness or otherwise of Waverley Abbey House for CWR. At this point, CWR's solicitor, Graham Ross-Cornes, put the case to the executor's representatives. They accepted the offer, with the wry comment: 'You must have someone up there working for you!'

Convinced, now, that God really had brought them to Waverley Abbey House, CWR paid a deposit of £81,000. The remainder was paid within several weeks through the gifts from God's people – much to the delight and amazement of the bank. If Selwyn, Trevor and their advisers had needed to exercise faith in the purchase of the house, even more was needed as they began to tackle the renovations.

'Nothing is too difficult for Thee'

As Enid's health deteriorated, Trevor took complete responsibility for the work at Waverley Abbey House. Selwyn was only involved at the executive level; everything else, including negotiations with the architects, the local authorities and the builders devolved on to Trevor. It was a massive job for him, made all the more difficult because of the many problems encountered while the refurbishing, rebuilding and redecoration work was in progress. As the house was a grade two star listed building, the major changes that were necessary had to be negotiated at every stage, only a limited number of changes would normally be allowed. Furthermore, the walls contained a large amount of wood and, because of dry rot, much of it had to be removed entirely. The extent of this problem was so daunting that one professional surveyor suggested that CWR should burn down the building, collect the insurance, and start all over again. This, in his view, would have been the most sensible course of action.

At one stage, the money for the project ran out, causing the laying off of the tradesmen. The arrival of a hoax cheque for £500,000 did nothing to lift Trevor's spirits – neither did the forging of a CWR cheque for £10,000 by one of the subcontractors. It was recovered – two years later.

Quite understandably, the burden of Trevor's task took its toll on his mental and physical energies. There were many moments of discouragement. Sometimes he felt quite disconsolate. On one such occasion, he took Debbie Hartland (later to become his wife) on a trip to Windsor Great Park. Lying there on the ground, he looked up into the heavens, feeling lethargic and almost tempted to give up on Waverley.

As he lay there, sprawled out on the grass, a family sat down nearby. The two boys started singing: 'Ah Lord God, Thou hast made the heavens . . .' with the refrain: 'Nothing is too difficult for Thee.' By the time they had sung it through several times, tears were running down Trevor's face. When he got up, he felt a new surge of strength, and ready to continue the work. The boys' timely singing of that chorus both affirmed the majesty and greatness of God and kindled fresh hope in his heart.

By the summer of 1987, Selwyn and Trevor were able to fix a date for the opening of the house and so to begin a new chapter in the history of CWR.

The official opening

In May 1987, Selwyn wrote to George Thomas – Lord Tonypandy – former Speaker of the House of Commons, inviting him to participate in the opening ceremony of Waverley Abbey House:

> The Crusade is an interdenominational organisation, 22 years old this coming August, which I founded in 1965. We are members of the Evangelical Alliance and are well-known in Christian circles.
>
> I am myself a Welshman, having been born and brought up near Dowlais, Glamorgan, and, after training in Bristol, entered the Christian ministry in 1950. The main purpose behind the founding of CWR was to encourage people to pray for a spiritual revival similar to that which shook Wales in past generations and to read the Scriptures daily. We have several publications geared to daily Bible reading and our leading publication EVERY DAY WITH JESUS is read worldwide by close on half a million people daily.
>
> We purchased Waverley Abbey House three years ago in order to establish it as a Christian training centre, prepared along the lines presented in the enclosed brochure. Eventually we plan to develop it into a Christian University but that is a long-term goal.
>
> We thought a good deal about who to invite to conduct

the actual opening ceremony and we thought it would be lovely to have someone like yourself, a Welshman, with a love of the Bible and a concern for Christian education.

We will be inviting local dignitaries and some Members of Parliament to the opening but we would very much like you, if you are free and feel able to accept this invitation, to conduct the actual opening ceremony.

The invitation was accepted with enthusiasm: 'I am quite excited at the development on which you have embarked, and it will be a great joy for me to come to you on Saturday, 29th August 1987.'

The Reverend Gilbert Kirby, former Principal of London Bible College, and Philip Hillsdon, a musician and friend of CWR, were also involved in the opening ceremony, along with Selwyn, Trevor and David Rivett. In his address, Selwyn described the occasion as 'an exciting and emotional event' in the history of CWR – a milestone. He also spoke of his gratitude to God for giving the organisation such an exquisite place as the base for future operations:

We are planting here today the seeds of a Christian university, although we may not see it for ten or fifteen years. It is a small start, but one we believe, down the years, will bear fruit to the honour and glory of God.

Lord Tonypandy was equally confident about Waverley Abbey House's future: 'This place will be a powerhouse for Jesus Christ in the unfolding years, which are yet to be revealed ... It will be used to train tomorrow's leaders in the Christian world, which will be so different from the world today. We can be sure of this – in a hundred years, when other folk will be here celebrating this day, the need of people and the challenge of the Gospel will be the same as it is now.'

Gratitude to God, a vision for the future, the vital need for the proclamation of the Gospel and for training the Christian leaders of future generations – these were keynotes struck by more than one speaker. It was a momentous and happy day,

Selwyn's one regret being that Enid was not there to share it with him.

However, he was greatly encouraged by the support of his guests. Hugh Fuller, of Kingsway Publications, wrote to thank him for a 'wonderful day', expressing his sense of privilege at being there: 'I am sure it was a landmark in the history of evangelical Christianity in this country.' He also remarked that he had 'never before seen any Christian building so tastefully presented'. The Reverend Tom Walker, General Superintendent of the Elim Pentecostal Church, wrote: 'This certainly is a milestone in the development of your work and ministry, and we offer to you our loving congratulations and our warmest greetings on this auspicious occasion.' Almost everyone remarked on the superb workmanship seen in every room in the house and the peaceful atmosphere radiating throughout the whole building. For many people, too, it was a day of real personal encouragement, giving them new hope for the future.

Throughout the purchase and renovation of the house, Selwyn and Trevor had sought God's guidance, through prayer and meditation, on all crucial decisions. They insisted on the highest possible standards for the house, since it was to be used for God's work, and the 1987 brochure stated that 'the entire training programme at Waverley Abbey House will be presented against the background of *a commitment to excellence*. This commitment is elegantly illustrated in the decor and fittings throughout the house, including the Lecture Hall, where modern equipment is available to enhance the speakers' presentations. Detailed and comprehensive surveys were drawn up for each stage of the work, including, most importantly, the financial requirements; this enabled the original 'vision' to become a reality. The generosity of CWR's friends and supporters also contributed to the establishment of its new base, thus making possible what Gilbert Kirby describes as 'a modern miracle'. Then there was the dynamic leadership of Trevor, who supervised the work single-handedly, for the most part. Without him, Waverley Abbey House would not have been as it is today.

Seminars, courses and retreats

Since August 1987, CWR has operated from two centres. The publishing division is based at Sunbury and is led by Geoff Booker. Geoff was formerly at Kingsway Publications, which had previously approached CWR about distributing *Every Day with Jesus* (see chapter 7). All the residential training courses (plus the administration relating to the courses and to CWR's Partners, a group of people committed to the ministry of CWR) are based at Waverley Abbey House. During its first year (1987–88), courses occupied 30 percent of the building, in the second (1988–89) 50 percent, the projected figure for 1989–90 being 86 percent.

The extent and variety of these courses and seminars is striking. For example, the 1990 schedule included:

Business and Professional Seminar

Christian Writers' Seminar

Counselling a Troubled Marriage Seminar

Counselling Youth Problems Seminar

Eating Disorders and Addictions Seminar

Educators' Seminar

Evangelism Seminar

Fostering and Adoption Seminar

House Group Leaders' Seminar

Institute of Biblical Studies

Institute of Christian Counselling

Lay Leadership and Church Workers' Seminar

Managing Redundancy Seminar

Man to Man Seminar

Marriage Enrichment Weekend

Medical Seminar

Meditation Retreat

Ministers and Christian Leaders' Institute

Personal Evangelism Seminar

Personal Growth Weekend

Planning a Fruitful Retirement Seminar

Prayer Retreats

Pre-marital Preparation Seminar

Producing Publicity Material Seminar

Psychological and Personality Problems Seminar

Sexual Abuse Seminar

School of Prayer

Singles' Seminar

Social Workers' Seminar

Team Dynamics Day

Women with Women Seminar

Youth Workers' and Leaders' Seminar

Vocational Guidance Seminar

Waverley Abbey House was described by a visitor at its opening as 'a jewel in the crown of evangelical Christianity'. To ensure that it continues to operate positively will require an equal amount of vision, hard work and dedication, as was required for its original development, and its secure financial foundation must be maintained for CWR's many ministries to grow and develop in the years ahead.

Sometime after the work on the house was completed, Selwyn and Trevor were having lunch at Waverley with the bank managers. 'Something worries us,' said one of them. 'From a business point of view, this operation relies heavily on the input of you two gentlemen. What would happen if you both were to die suddenly?' After a pause, Selwyn responded: 'Gentlemen, the enterprise we belong to is a far greater concern than even Barclays Bank. What you see here is just a small part of the Church Universal. It is not dependent on us. Should the Lord call us to be with Him, He will raise other people to continue His work here in this place.' There was a moment's silence, an embarrassed look ... and the conversation was hurriedly moved along.

Selwyn committed himself almost exclusively to Waverley

for the first two years of its ministry. This meant exceptionally strict management of his time and energy. His schedule for a three-week period in the autumn of 1989 read like this:

Friday to Sunday	Pre-marriage Weekend
Monday to Thursday	Residential Counselling Course
Friday to Sunday	Marriage Enrichment Course
Monday	Writing
Tuesday	Administration and meetings
Wednesday	Writing
Thursday	Aministration and meetings
Friday	Writing
Saturday and Sunday	Medical Seminar Weekend (three lectures)

Organising his time is a matter of self-discipline – under the direction of the Holy Spirit. He has to make sacrifices and his social life is almost non-existent. Sometimes on his own for long periods, particularly when writing, he has become self-sufficient, dealing with his own feelings and worries without recourse to close friends. Since Enid's illness, when he did not feel he could burden her with his emotions, he has become accustomed to this way of life.

With the house well-established, Selwyn now planned to expand his ministry (and that of CWR) by travelling more extensively than he has done for many years. The opening of Waverley Abbey House was not an end in itself, rather the beginning of an even greater outreach for Selwyn, Trevor and CWR.

One of the reasons for this is that Selwyn is regarded by experts as one of the foremost proponents of Biblical counselling in Britain. There is a Scriptural basis to his work reminiscent of Lawrence Crabb's approach: 'Every concept of Biblical counselling must build upon the fundamental premise that there really is an infinite and personal God who has revealed Himself propositionally in the written word, the Bible, and personally in the living word, Jesus Christ.'

Lawrence Crabb is a Christian psychologist based in Colorado, USA, where he has a training college in Biblical counselling. Selwyn spent some time with him when in the USA and was profoundly impressed by his strong Biblical approach.

The hallmarks of Selwyn's approach to counselling are an absolute belief in the Bible as 'divinely inspired and without error in all its parts' and a discriminating use of secular therapies, the goal of all his counselling being to move the client from self-centredness to Christ-centredness.

Like Lawrence Crabb, Selwyn offers counselling at three levels – encouragement, exhortation and enlightenment. This approach is a fundamental part of CWR's Regional Counsellor Training Programme. This programme operates on a three-tier system. Initially, ministers and church leaders are brought together in an area for a one-day conference to explain CWR's approach to Christian counselling. Next, a basic one-day seminar, 'Caring by Encouragement' is held, to which all are invited. This seminar is designed to help people understand the simple principles of Christian caring. Those who go through this seminar will then be able to attend a further seminar, 'Caring by Exhortation', which is held some weeks later in the same area. This focuses on the use of Biblical principles to help people with their problems. Those wanting to go on to an even deeper level will then be able to attend a 'Caring by Enlightenment' seminar which gives insights on how to help people unravel the incorrect thinking and wrong beliefs that often lie behind stubborn and difficult problems. Those who have attended all three seminars will then be entitled, with their minister's recommendation, to apply for the Counselling Course, which is presented on video, so making possible training sessions for smaller groups in more local areas.

Chapter Eleven

FACING
THE FUTURE

*. . . walking by the light
of a true relationship –
every day with Jesus*

Selwyn Hughes and CWR look to the future with eager anticipation and confidence. Selwyn still works energetically and with as much verve and enjoyment as ever. His creative flow of ideas shows no sign of abating, neither has he any fear for what may lie ahead. Having proved, from day to day, that God is absolutely reliable, he is quite sure that His grace will be sufficient:

It is, of course, gratifying to think that one can live on in the thoughts and lives of those to whom we have been a good influence, but there is a far richer consolation offered to those who truly know Christ. His offer of life after death is founded, not just on a belief but on a demonstration – the resurrection of Jesus from the dead.[1]

However, we must not become complacent, for the Church is often prayerless, harshly critical, unloving and unrepentant. How can it grow unless men and women are challenged to truly *repent* as they begin their Christian lives, and are shown the continuing need of an on-going repentance. Selwyn is concerned at the number of argumentative, self-centred and rebellious believers in the Church: '. . . when any issue comes up between their will and God's will,' he writes, 'they, never having learned the way of obedience and repentance, take a self-centred stance.' Since this will usually be in opposition to God's stance, what hope is there for a Church that is already in decline? Every year, every denomination reports waning numbers and the Church's influence in the world is continually shrinking. That's why Selwyn warns us against any false optimism:

The patient may have all the outward signs of good health, but when proper tests are given, the results show cause for deep concern. Don't be misled, I beg you, by the sabre rattling that goes on in today's Church. We sing, we shout, we hold occasional large meetings and conferences, but when it is all over, what impact have we made on society? Some perhaps, but far less than we ought. 'Success,' said someone, 'is measured not by what we are, but by what we are, compared to what we could be.' All the good we accomplish is nothing compared to what needs to be accomplished. The world laughs at our attempts to influence it. It sees us as weak, feeble and ineffectual. *It is time to seek the Lord.*[2]

Selwyn is determined that CWR should continue to play its part in the process of 'seeking the Lord' – an essential prerequisite for revival.

Looking back now over the early and middle years of his life, Selwyn is conscious of God's hand shaping many varied experiences in order to bring him to his present understanding. With more than a trace of egotism, he entitled his autobiography (written in 1963, before the start of CWR), *Walking With Destiny*. Yet this title, with its Churchillian overtones, points away from the man himself to the reality of God's guiding presence.

Relationships

Success has not come easily. It hasn't dropped from heaven. Selwyn has had to work extremely hard, honing his natural gifts and skills so as to achieve maximum effectiveness, particularly in the area of relationships. In his relationships he has learned to adjust to the needs of those working for and with him, becoming more sympathetic as a result. Before CWR was founded, few people had worked with Selwyn for any length of time. In the early days of his ministry, he was difficult – and individualist, a 'driven' man, a loner, an uneasy colleague, whose primary interest was his *own* ministry. Not always alive to the feelings of others, there was an inevitability about the conflict in Sheffield in 1958.

Gradually, however, as Selwyn came to understand himself more thoroughly – both as a person and as a minister – he became a more 'complete' person. Skill joined to dedication has made him considerably effective. Impatience, pride and hot-headedness were replaced by calm. A humble realisation of his true worth has brought a more balanced approach to his life and family, and to many other people and churches.

David, Selwyn's older son, recalls that he has always enjoyed 'a very good relationship' with his father: they talk freely and mutually swop ideas. He gives his considered view of Selwyn as a man, father and grandfather:

As a *father* he was steady and dependable: I always knew where I was with him. He was not moody, his attitudes were consistent. He was a thoroughly good father, always ready to help and advise me. I was, however, closer to my mother. She was always there while my father was frequently away preaching and teaching. I didn't regret his absences because he was doing what he felt called to do; my mother accepted it calmly, so why shouldn't I? Selwyn and Enid were deeply in love and the only time I recall my father crying was on the day of her death. He was clearly under great strain in the years before her death, but handled it well.

As a *grandfather* he is friendly, loving, but doesn't get to see the grandchildren often because of pressure of work.

As a *man* he is obviously a leader, with a clear understanding of people and their problems. He is a self-contained person who doesn't like big family gatherings, preferring instead small and more intimate occasions. He's not concerned with possessions, hates gardening, likes the theatre and swimming (if the water's hot), and particularly things American, including visiting that country. He also enjoys watching snooker, Max Boyce (the Welsh commedian), and the Welsh rugby team, especially when they are winning.

Three influences were paramount in the development, over the years, of Selwyn's understanding of relationships. There was his conception of family life and the role model offered by his father, derived from his childhood in South Wales. Added to this is his lifelong reading of the Bible which, as he rightly says, is occupied with relationships from beginning to end. Thirdly, he gained many insights from his reading of Lawrence Crabb's writings. Selwyn continually seeks to apply Biblical insights and Biblical psychology in a practical, attainable way. His advice is eminently sensible and pastoral – always encouraging but also realistic. He remains open and willing to learn.

Through his experiences of life, Selwyn has perceived the Holy Spirit's influence: directing, cajoling, purifying. He has *submitted* himself to the Spirit: 'So having the Holy Spirit within is not just being the recipient of pleasurable emotions - it is being a better person.' By 'better', he means exhibiting the fruit of the Spirit (love, joy, peace, good temper, kindliness, generosity, fidelity, gentleness, self-control) in every-day life. A Christian is called to reveal both purity and power in his relationships, not as a result of human effort, but of the direct, supernatural presence of the Holy Spirit.

Trevor's arrival forced Selwyn to work at his relationships, bringing the whole area into sharp relief. From this time on, relationships took on great spiritual significance to him, simply because 'to be, is to be in relationships'. Selwyn defines relationships as 'the ability to connect with people' in a meaningful, creative way. Christianity, itself, has its beginnings in a relationship, since the disciples were called to be 'with Jesus'. Today each person's relationship with Him, according to Selwyn, is 'the fountain from which every good flows. Trying to 'be good' without that relationship is like trying to get a stream without a spring, or sunlight without the sun. Anything that hinders the relationship with Him blocks everything that flows from the relationship. Everything.' Relationships are prominent in Scripture because 'only in the context of relationships can the deepest longings of our being be met and satisfied'. Without them, there can be no growth, spiritual or physical. God has so designed us that we *need* each other.

The way we view ourselves is the result of our early relationships and, all too often, people carry emotional scars, inflicted during childhood, into adult life. Selwyn cites this example:

A forty-year-old woman, who was having difficulties in her marriage relationship, told me: 'I used to sit on the stairs at night and listen to my mother and father talking about me. They said such things as, "What a painful and pitiful child our daughter is; thank goodness she is out of the way." This woman carried those voices that came out of that early relationship into her marriage, and they gave her a view of herself which made it difficult for her to give herself to her husband or to have any optimism about her future. Her relationships shaped her life – until she learned how to see herself from God's point of view.[3]

Children build up their basic pictures of God from those adults who play a leading part in their early lives. They may receive an *intellectual* view of God from the Bible verses they hear in Sunday School or at church, but this will be of secondary importance to the way their own parents relate to them on an every-day basis. Selwyn has discovered that many problems in adult life stem from a wrong concept of God:

> And when I've probed to find out where this wrong concept has come from, nine times out of ten, I've discovered that it has come from their earliest relationships with their mother or father, because most of us will relate to God in the way we related to our parents – especially our fathers.[4]

Like Dr E. Stanley Jones, the famous missionary, Selwyn believes that we are as mature as our relationships. A person who is able to relate to others in love has a high level of maturity, but one who continually retreats into himself, becoming increasingly self-preoccupied is immature. The truly well-adjusted person will not only relate well to others, but also be in tune with himself and with God. Sin works against good relationships by producing estrangement: 'estrangement from God, estrangement from ourselves and estrangement from others.'

Relationships within the Christian church are distinctive. They are rooted in the fact that God took the initiative, breaking down all the barriers between Him and us. The quality of this special relationship He sets up with us, Selwyn believes, should then be carried into our relationships with others. If we don't do this, we have to accept the blame – the breakdown of a relationship is caused by our negligence. God has told us specifically that the greatest commandment for any Christian is that we should love God and our neighbour as ourself. Until God, Himself, came into the world, we had no example to follow, but now we have no such excuse. We are to love as Christ loved.

Selwyn points out that Christ loved the disciples *not* as they loved themselves and each other, but with a new, different kind of love: 'A love that required a new word to express it – *agape.*' Selwyn pours his heart into making this fact plain:

Love for God was the foundation on which the Ten Commandments were constructed. It was embodied in the very elements of God's principles for human life from the beginning. But then John adds a fascinating phrase: "Yet I am writing you a new command; its truth is seen in him and you ..." (v.8: NIV). Was John thinking here of the statement of Jesus in John 13:34, "A new command I give you: love one another. As I have loved you, so you must love one another" (NIV)? I think so.

That last phrase of Jesus, "As I have loved you", lifted the commandment from the Old Testament to the New, from law to grace. The mystery of love would never really have been understood by this world unless Jesus had come and demonstrated it by His words, by His deeds and by His death. The word would have been barren had not Jesus filled it with the content of the purest and highest love this world has ever seen. "Love one another *as I have loved you*" is the high watermark in the history of mankind. Jesus made it clear what love really is by putting into the word the content of His own character. Such was the revelation that it required a new word to express it – agape. "As I have loved you" becomes the standard of loving for the whole universe. There is nothing higher.[5]

Every day, in many different respects, we have to choose between self-protection and trust. It was a revelation to Selwyn when he came to realise how consistently he opted for self-protection in his relationships with others. He would allow people close enough to affirm him, but not so close that they might hurt him. Lawrence Crabb's writings on this helped Selwyn as he sought to start afresh, wiping away all the painful memories of past disappointments.

Eventually, Selwyn saw that to love is to hold others in the highest esteem. In practical terms, this means choosing to move outwards, *towards* another person, rather than away from them into oneself. We have to maintain this movement towards others in the face of all rejection – even as our Lord did when we treated Him with such disdain during His time on earth.

Anxious to convey to others all that he has learned, Selwyn offers five practical steps towards right relationships within our churches:

1. Face reality and acknowledge your inadequacies in this area.
2. Remember that 'agape' love is our natural response to God's love for us.
3. Put yourself, deliberately, in a position where you risk being hurt.
4. Meet together in small groups convened with the express purpose of giving and receiving feedback.
5. Focus on the fact that when you relate properly to others, you enable them to have a clearer and more comprehensive understanding of God.

Looking ahead

Secure in its relationships, CWR can face the future resolutely. In purely financial terms, it has a solid platform from which to launch its long-term objectives and developments. The three Executive Directors – Selwyn, Trevor and David – are men with different, though complementary, gifts. All three recognise that constant vigilance is needed to ensure the future effectiveness of the ministry. Above all, they – plus their staff at Waverley Abbey House and Sunbury – share a common vision for the future.

This is threefold. First, it includes a deep concern for the church. One of the strengths of CWR's ministry has been its application of the Christian faith to the practical aspects of daily living, showing the relevance of the Scriptures to everyday circumstances. This down-to-earth approach will continue to be demonstrated, in the years ahead, through the teaching and training seminars and courses, designed to equip men and women for maximum effectiveness within the Church; through the establishment of a Christian counselling centre, to minister directly to those who are in deep need; and through a daily prayer ministry, taking place in a part of Waverley Abbey House that has been specially adapted for this purpose. A research and resource centre will research topics of vital interest to Christian workers in order to provide up-to-date information in printed form; national rallies will be held in strategic cities all over Britain, while retreats and conferences will be held to discuss important issues affecting the life of the Church.

Secondly, CWR feels a responsibility for the spiritual health of the nation. Its goal is to train people who can make a powerful contribution to the life of Britain through their position or employment by integrating Biblical principles into their professions, which is why CWR hopes to establish a Christian College of Education. The courses presented at this college will show teachers, lawyers, and other professions, how to apply Biblical principles to their vocation to bring the light of Scripture into their situations. Once this college has been set up, it will become the foundation on which a Christian university will later be developed. The aim of this would counter the rationalistic and humanistic philosophies upon which so much of today's society is based. Another proposal is to develop 'CWR TV', a weekend television station coming direct from Waverly Abbey House. Programmes would be for the whole family, as well as being strongly evangelistic. An evangelistic team will be brought together to present the Gospel in a traditional as well as a contemporary format, using street theatre, music, mime and drama.

Finally, Selwyn and his fellow workers believe that in the next decade CWR's ministry will extend beyond the shores of Britain in a way not previously seen in the past 25 years. There will be four major strands to this outreach:

1. **The Ambassador Programme**
   This will train personnel to take abroad the ministry of *Every Day with Jesus* to establish a national 'ministry base' which will be responsible for distributing CWR's materials and organising teaching seminars, conferences and crusades.

2. **The Sponsorship Programme**
   This will bring to Britain, under a special scholarship arrangement, men and women from abroad for training in such areas as leadership, counselling and administration. Having received this training, they will return to their own countries to share the knowledge and expertise they have gained.

3. **Translations and translators**
   During the next ten years, it is CWR's intention to translate *Every Day with Jesus*, and some of the other publications, into as many languages as possible.

4. **Satellite television**
   There may be an opening for Satellite TV through Europe's New World Channel. CWR will do everything it can to present as many television programmes as possible through this.

Selwyn will be closely involved with all these challenging and exciting initiatives, Waverley Abbey House remaining the focal point of a teaching, training and ministry programme, aimed at producing people of character and integrity who are capable of changing contemporary society. It is a prospect that thrills Selwyn. At some point in the future, perhaps, he would like a leadership role in a local church. He has always remained a preacher and pastor at heart, in spite of his many years away from a local pastoral ministry. Such a move would not be unduly detrimental to the overall work of CWR. Trevor Partridge has all the ability needed for guiding the work of CWR into the next century.

These further changes may be many years into the future

but, no doubt, Selwyn will recognise the moment for decisive change, and his timing will be as right as it has been with all the other crucial decisions affecting his life. He will prepare for changes intelligently and prayerfully, with the confidence that God is working creatively in his life. As with all other major aspects of his life, it is difficult to escape the conclusion that Selwyn is a man who has walked with destiny; and all these years he has been walking by the light of a true relationship – every day with Jesus.

Appendix

THE 'DYNAMIC CHRISTIAN LIVING' SEMINAR

The seminar is an intensive eight-hour course of study, designed to identify the basic biblical principles which underlie all effective Christian living, and upon which all Christian experience is built. It attempts to bridge the gap between belief and behaviour. It stresses the importance of relating what we believe to how we live, and that the truth of God's Word is meant to be a working reality in our every day lives and experience.

The whole course consists of eight sessions organised in the following way:

Session One – Design for Living

This session centres on God's design in man (Genesis 1:26–27) and His order for successful living: the proper balance of spirit, soul and body, in relation to the worlds of the spiritual and the physical. Against this design, of course, there is Satan's counter-attack, intended to upset the balance God has built within man (Genesis 2:16–17). God's response to this, as the session shows so clearly, is that Christ has come as God's plan for the removal of sin, guilt, pride, ego-centricity, etc.

Session Two – Seeing Ourselves in Christ

The second session shows that once Christ has been admitted to a person's life, the process of becoming like Him begins (Romans 8:29). Maturity is developed by God's Word, with its four-fold thrust of doctrine, reproof, correction and instruction (2 Timothy 3:17, A.V.). Importantly the session indicates that surface problems in our Christian experience are often the symptoms of a wrong basic attitude which has never been resolved in a Scriptural way.

Session Three – Inner Harmony

This session is concerned with the fact that, sooner or later, the Christian realises that although he had experienced conversion, there are still deep problems within his personality: lust, jealousy, hostility, anxiety, depression and doubt. It shows too that as Christ is allowed to live within our beings He is free to work with the Holy Spirit to deepen our characters, overcome our conflicts and elevate our lives to the level of His own. Then it goes on to deal with a clear conscience, stating the view that as Christians we should regularly check areas of our lives to see that conscience has not been violated:

I must ask myself

Have I lied to anyone and never taken steps to correct it?

Have I stolen anything from anyone and never remedied the matter?

Have I lost my temper with anyone and not yet apologised?

Have I damaged the reputation of anyone and failed to take the steps to correct the situation?

Have I rebelled against those over me in authority (school, work, the home) and have not put things right?

Have I grieved God (and others) by my ingratitude?

Have I committed fornication, adultery, or any other sexual sin and not yet sought forgiveness?

Have I violated God's laws by dabbling in fortune telling, spiritism, playing with the ouija board, etc.?

Am I harbouring bitterness against God because of unanswered prayer?

Am I holding resentment against another who has wronged me and I won't forgive?

The steps which help a person towards a clear conscience are also highlighted.

Session Four – Turning Setbacks into Springboards

The theme of this part of the course is that one of the greatest discoveries we can make in the Christian experience is to understand whenever God permits anything to happen it is because He sees a way whereby He can use that situation for His further praise and glory. To discover how God can turn the seeming set-backs of life into springboards of new discoveries is one of the most revolutionary concepts of dynamic Christian living.

Session Five – Getting the Best Out of the Bible

This deals with the art of meditation, and shows that as the Word of God saturates our minds, the thought patterns in our minds which have been built up and are contrary to Him are broken up. 'Meditation', says this session, 'is the applying of truth as a working reality in our daily living'.

Session Six – Discovering God's Will and Purpose For Our Lives

This session deals honestly but sensitively with discovering our place within the Body of Christ, and is largely concerned with the gifts we may exercise as described in

   (a) Romans 12: the gifts of the Lord

   (b) 1 Corinthians 12: the gifts of the Holy Spirit

   (c) Ephesians 4: the gifts of Christ.

    It also has a most useful checklist for determining the Will of God:

1. Have I consulted God's Word on this matter?
2. Am I seeking what I want or what God wants?
3. Is there any known disobedience in my life which will prevent me from receiving the direction I need?
4. Have I taken the necessary steps to widen my sensitivity to the voice of God?
5. What is my basic motivation in this matter?
6. Is there a spiritual person with whom I can confer on this matter?
7. Have I applied the principle of 'the way of peace'?
8. Will it demand compromise?
9. Do the Word of God, the witness of the Holy Spirit, and circumstances fall clearly in line?
10. Will it help conform me to God's highest ideal for my life – to be like Jesus?

Session Seven – Right Relationships

The last but one session stresses the importance of communicating effectively with each person we, as Christians, encounter. It pays particular attention to right relationships within courtship and marriage. It culminates with an analysis of the whole meaning of genuine love:

1. **THIS LOVE OF WHICH WE SPEAK IS SLOW TO LOSE PATIENCE**
   Has no irritation and knows how to make problems work toward further development.

2. **IT LOOKS FOR A WAY OF BEING CONSTRUCTIVE**
   Genuine love is able to recognise the needs of the other person. It designs ways in which the other can be benefited.

3. **IT IS NOT POSSESSIVE**
   Allows freedom for the other person to develop fulfilment without objection or jealousy.

4. **IT IS NEITHER ANXIOUS TO IMPRESS**
   Is not interested in making an impression or projecting a self-image for purely personal gain.

5. **DOES NOT CHERISH INFLATED IDEAS OF ITS OWN IMPORTANCE**
   It does not expect life to revolve around itself and is flexible to the ideas of others.

6. **LOVE HAS GOOD MANNERS**
   Respects others and knows how to do the right thing.

7. **IT DOES NOT PURSUE SELFISH ADVANTAGE**
   Does not make its primary concern the satisfaction of personal appetites, but has concern for the needs of the other person.

8. **IT IS NOT TOUCHY**
   Not easily hurt. Does not get too emotionally involved with personal opinions so as to reject the person who gives them.

9. **IT DOES NOT KEEP AN ACCOUNT OF EVIL**
   Doesn't review wrongs and reflect upon them but destroys the evidence of past mistakes. Forgives – and forgets.

10. **DOES NOT GLOAT OVER THE WICKEDNESS OF OTHERS**
    Doesn't use other people's failures to excuse oneself.

---

11. **IS GLAD WITH ALL GODLY MEN WHEN TRUTH PREVAILS**
    Is interested in the spiritual objectives of all people.

12. **KNOWS NO LIMIT TO ITS FORBEARANCE**
    Is able to live with the faults and failings of others.

13. **THERE IS NO END TO ITS TRUST**
    Believes in a person's worth, does not doubt integrity.

14. **NO FADING OF ITS HOPE**
    Enjoys a perfect peace that God can work through all things.

15. **IT HAS UNLIMITED ENDURANCE**
    Outlasts everything – loves on even when love is unreciprocated.

Session Eight – Conformed To His Image

Its central theme is that God's plan for individual lives is to accomplish His specific purpose through us so that when we finish our life's work we can say like Christ 'I have finished the work which you gave me to do'. Put another way, it means that Jesus Christ works to re-live His life through us, replacing pride and ego with inward humility and poverty in spirit; replacing insensitivity with deep sensitivity; replacing anger and impatience with meek and joyful submission; replacing apathy and indifference with a deep spiritual hunger; replacing bitterness and resentment with a merciful and willing forgiveness; replacing impurity and uncleanness with purity of heart, mind and action; replacing condemnation and criticism with a peaceful desire to bring about harmony; replacing fear and compromise with a positive identification of what Christ expects of us.

It also has a chart for evaluating our monthly spiritual progress:

Secret pride of face, grace, place, race	
Stiffness and preciseness	
Love of praise: hurt feelings	
Fondness to be noticed	
Love of supremacy	
Stirring of anger or impatience	
Nervous tension, called 'holy indignation'	
Love of the world – its pleasures and possessions	
Throwing sharp words – Disposition to retaliate	
Self-will; stubborness	
Unteachable spirit	
Overtalkativeness; undue lack of quietness	
Sarcastic, peevish, fretful spirit	
Headstrong, wilful	
Driving, commanding, demanding attitude	
Picking flaws, back-biting	
Love to be coaxed	
Fear of man	
Shirking duty: alibis, procrastination	
Compromising convictions rather than standing firm	
Jealousy, envy, deceit	
Covering one's own faults	
Leaving a better impression than is true	
Unbelief, unfaithful to spiritual tasks	
Discouragement, glum, self-centred	
Worry, complaining with man and God	
Lack of concern for the unsaved	
Love of ease – Love of money	
Little desire for God's Word – No time alone with God	

References

Introduction

1. *Every Day with Jesus*, 7th September 1987. CWR: Sunbury on Thames.
2. Ibid., 2nd September 1987.
3. *News Update* No. 15. CWR: Sunbury on Thames.
4. Ibid.
5. Ibid.
6. Interview at Waverley Abbey House.
7. *Every Day with Jesus*, February/March 1989 edition.
8. *Every Day with Jesus*, September/October 1987 edition.
9. Interview in *Renewal*, May 1988, p. 8 ff.
10. *Every Day with Jesus*, 30 May 1989.

Chapter One

1. Hughes, Selwyn. *Walking with Destiny* (p. 12). CWR: London, 1965.
2. Ibid. (p. 5).
3. Whittaker, Colin. *Seven Pentecostal Pioneers* (pp. 53–54). Marshall Pickering: Basingstoke, 1983.
4. *Walking with Destiny* (p. 6).
5. Ibid. (p. 7).
6. Ibid. (pp. 7–8).

Chapter Two

1. *Walking with Destiny* (p. 12)
2. *Every Day with Jesus*, 28th July 1989.
3. Hughes, Selwyn. *Sharing your Faith* (pp. 4–5). Marshall Pickering: Basingstoke, 1981.
4. *Walking with Destiny* (p. 14).
5. Ibid. (pp. 15–16).
6. Ibid. (p. 17).
7. Ibid. (pp. 17–18).
8. Ibid. (p. 18).
9. John 1:29 says: 'The next day John saw Jesus coming towards him and said, "Look the Lamb of God, who takes away the sin of the world"'; while John 1:33 says: 'The man on whom you see the Spirit come down and remain is he who will baptise with the Holy Spirit'.

10. *Walking with Destiny* (pp. 21–22)

11. Hughes, Selwyn. *A New Heart* (p. 32). Kingsway Publications: Eastbourne, 1982.

12. Ibid. (p. 33).

13. Ibid. (p. 34).

14. Ibid. (pp. 34–35).

15. Ibid. (p. 35).

16. *Sharing your Faith* (pp. 17–18).

17. England, Edward (Ed.). *My Call to Preach* (p. 114). Highland Books: Crowborough, 1986.

18. Ibid. (pp. 14–15).

19. Ibid. (pp. 116–117).

20. Ibid. (p. 117).

21. *Walking with Destiny* (pp. 23–24).

22. Ibid. (p. 32).

23. Ibid. (p. 33–34).

Chapter Three

1. *Sharing your Faith* (pp. 17–18).

2. Hughes, Selwyn. 'Communicating His love' in *My Call to Preach* (p. 114).

3. *Walking with Destiny* (p. 32).

4. Ibid. (p. 40).

Chapter Four

1. Hughes, Selwyn. *God Wants You Whole* (pp. 11–12). Kingsway Publications: Eastbourne, 1984.

2. Ibid. (p. 13).

3. *Walking with Destiny* (p. 40).

4. Ibid. (pp. 46–47).

5. Ibid. (pp. 46–47).

6. Ibid. (pp. 52–53).

Chapter Five

1. *Walking with Destiny* (pp. 63–65).

2. Ibid. (pp. 63–65).

3. Ibid. (pp. 63–65).

References

Chapter Six

1. This postcard was found in September 1989 when staff were clearing out files from CWR's old Weybridge office.

Chapter Seven

1. The material in this chapter is based largely on interviews at Waverley Abbey House with Selwyn Hughes and Trevor Partridge.

Chapter Eight

1. *Every Day with Jesus*, 10th January 1988.
2. Ibid., 18th February 1987.
3. Ibid., 28th January 1987.
4. Ibid., 24th May 1985.
5. Ibid., 4th September 1988.
6. Ibid., 4th November 1983.
7. Ibid., 2nd June 1986.
8. Ibid., 27th November 1985.
9. Ibid., 17th June 1987.

Chapter Nine

1. The material here is primarily based on Selwyn's recollections, together with those of Enid's sister, Mrs Joan Williams, who still lives in Helston, Cornwall.
2. I am grateful to Trevor Partridge for giving me complete access to the notes of his address at Enid's funeral.

Chapter Eleven

1. *Every Day with Jesus*, 22nd March 1987.
2. Ibid., 22nd January 1984.
3. Ibid., 13th November 1989.
4. Ibid., 16th November 1989.
5. Ibid., 12th December 1983.
6. Ibid., 8th December 1989.